MW01110380

Mediterranean Diet:

100+ Mediterranean Diet Recipes & Desserts You Can Cook At Home! (Mediterranean Diet Cookbook, Lose Weight, Heart Healthy, Fight Disease & Slow Aging)

Kevin Gise © 2017

Disclaimer:

This book is for informational purposes only and the author, his agents, heirs, and assignees do not accept any responsibilities for any liabilities, actual or alleged, resulting from the use of this information.

This report is not "professional advice." The author encourages the reader to seek advice from a professional where any reasonably prudent person would do so. While every reasonable attempt has been made to verify the information contained in this eBook, the author and his affiliates cannot assume any responsibility for errors, inaccuracies or omissions, including omissions in transmission or reproduction.

Any references to people, events, organizations, or business entities are for educational and illustrative purposes only, and no intent to falsely characterize, recommend, disparage, or injure is intended or should be so construed. Any results stated or implied are consistent with general results, but this means results can and will vary. The author, his agents, and assigns, make no promises or guarantees, stated or implied. Individual results will vary and this work is supplied strictly on an "at your own risk" basis.

Introduction

First off, thanks for purchasing my book "Mediterranean Diet: 100+ Mediterranean Diet Recipes & Desserts You Can Cook At Home! (Mediterranean Diet Cookbook, Lose Weight, Heart Healthy, Fight Disease & Slow Aging)". By grabbing this book you've shown that you're serious about trying out this diet and seeing if you can maintain a healthy lifestyle. This book will provide you with a bunch of delicious recipes to help you get started. I hope this diet has the same positive impact on your life that it did on those of my family and friends. They lost a ton of weight and have never felt healthier.

I'll be sharing over 100+ recipes I've gathered over the years. It's important before beginning any diet you check with your physician or doctor. The Mediterranean diet might not be right for everyone. The idea here is to get healthier. The last thing I'd want to see happen is you follow a diet that isn't helping you make positive progress towards that goal. I'm not a physician, I'm just a person who believes in the transformative power of the Mediterranean diet. I've seen the positive changes it can make in a person's life and I want to see that same positive change for all of you.

I hope you enjoy all the different recipes I've included. They should allow you to eat well for the foreseeable future.

I'm excited to begin. Let's get started!

Chapter One: Mediterranean Diet Breakfast Recipes

In this section, I will give you 25+ Mediterranean breakfast recipes you can make yourself. I'll include a few basic recipes and a few more advanced recipes. That way no matter what your level in the kitchen you'll be able to prepare yourself a heart-healthy Mediterranean meal to keep you on track with your diet.

My Big Fat Greek Omelet (Serves 4)

<u>Ingredients:</u>

8 Large Eggs

1 teaspoon of Dried Oregano

10 ounces of Frozen Chopped Spinach

1 cup of Grape Tomatoes

1 tablespoon of Olive Oil

1/2 cup of Crumbled Feta Cheese

1/2 teaspoon of Salt

Black Pepper

Directions:

1. Heat your skillet over a low heat. In your small-sized bowl, mix your tomatoes, 1/4 teaspoon of salt, 1/2 teaspoon of oregano, and pepper. Stir in your feta cheese.

2. In your medium-sized bowl, whisk together your eggs, stir in your spinach, 1/4 teaspoon of salt, 1/2 teaspoon of oregano, and pepper.

3. Add your oil to your pan and increase the heat to a medium-high. Add your egg mix to your skillet. Push back your eggs that set and let the uncooked eggs run onto the empty portion of your pan. Continue to do this until all of the eggs are fully cooked and moist. Reduce your heat to low and pour your tomato mixture over half of your omelet.

4. Fold the untopped half of your omelet over the filling. Slide your omelet from the pan onto your cutting board. Allow it to rest for a minute so the filling can warm.

5. Cut the omelet into 4 wedges.

6. Serve!

Red Pepper & Baked Egg Galettes (Serves 4)

Ingredients:

4 Large Fresh Eggs

2 Small Onions (Halved & Cut Into 1/2-Inch Wedges)

4 Small Red Bell Peppers (Cut Into 1/2-Inch Strips)

1 teaspoon of Cumin

1 sheet of Thawed Puff Pastry

6 tablespoon of Olive Oil

1 teaspoon of Coriander

12 teaspoons of Sour Cream

Handful of Chopped Fresh Parsley

Handful of Chopped Cilantro

Fresh Sprigs of Thyme (Leaves Removed)

1 Beaten Egg (For Brushing Pastry)

Salt

Fresh Cracked Pepper

Directions:

1. Set your oven to 400 degrees.

2. Mix together your pepper, thyme, onions, spices in your bowl. Add your olive oil and toss well so that everything is coated with your oil and spices.

3. Spread mixture on your baking sheet and roast for approximately 30 minutes, stirring and rearranging your vegetables a few times so they don't get burned.

4. Sprinkle your vegetables with half of your fresh herbs and set to the side.

6. Turn your oven up to 425 degrees. Roll out your pastry on a floured surface until it reaches a 12x12-inch square. Cut into four 6-inch squares. Transfer to 2 parchment or Silpat lined baking sheets.

7. Take your dull knife and score a small 1/4-inch frame around each square of your pastry. Don't cut all the way through. Prick the inside of your squares all over with the tines of your fork. Put back in your fridge for around 30 minutes.

8. Remove your pastry from your fridge and brush all over with your beaten egg. Spread the inside of each square with 3 teaspoons of your sour cream.

9. Top each with some of your vegetable mixture, spread it out evenly, leaving your borders free, and leaving a shallow depression in the center for the egg, which will go in later.

10. Bake for approximately 10 minutes until rising and starting to brown.

11. Remove and carefully crack your egg into the center of each galette.

12. Put back into your oven for approximately 10 minutes until your egg is set.

13. Sprinkle with your salt, pepper, and remaining herbs. Drizzle with some olive oil.

14. Serve!

Greek Omelet (Serves 2)

Ingredients:

4 Large Eggs

1/2 cup of Crumbled Feta Cheese

1/4 cup of Cooked Spinach

2 Thinly Sliced Scallions

2 tablespoons of Chopped Fresh Dill

2 teaspoons of Extra-Virgin Olive Oil

Ground Pepper

Directions:

1. Squeeze your spinach to remove any of the excess water. Blend your eggs with a fork in your bowl. Add your scallions, dill, feta, pepper, and spinach. Gently mix them together with your rubber spatula.

2. Preheat your broiler. Place your rack about 4-inches away from the heat source.

3. Heat your oil in your skillet over a medium heat. Pour your egg mixture into your skillet and tilt it to distribute it evenly. Reduce your heat to a medium-low and cook mixture until the bottom has turned a light golden color. Be sure to lift up the edges to allow any uncooked eggs to flow in underneath. Should take approximately 3 to 4 minutes.

4. Place your pan under your broiler and cook egg mixture until the top has set. This should take an additional 1 to 3 minutes.

5. Remove omelet from your pan and cut into wedges.

6. Serve!

Cheesy Mediterranean Scramble (Serves 6)

Ingredients:

6 slices of Whole Wheat Bread

3 cartons of Egg Substitute

1/2 teaspoon of Crushed Dried Basil Leaves

2 tablespoons of Low Fat Feta Cheese

1 1/2 tablespoons of Butter Spread

1 Small Chopped Sweet Onion

1 Small Chopped Red Pepper

1/8 teaspoon of Ground Black Pepper

Directions:

1. In your large-sized bowl add your egg substitute, black pepper, and basil. Whisk and set to the side.

2. In your 10-inch skillet, melt your butter spread over a medium-high heat and cook your onion and red pepper. Stir occasionally for 4 minutes until your vegetables get tender. Stir in your egg mixture and allow it to set slightly.

3. Cook your eggs until set, stirring occasionally. Sprinkle with your cheese. Toast your slices of white bread.

4. Serve!

Greek Scramble (Serves 4)

Ingredients:

10 Large Eggs

2/3 cup of Crumbled Feta Cheese

1/4 cup of Milk

1 tablespoon of Olive Oil

6 ounces of Baby Spinach

1 cup of Quartered Cherry Tomatoes

1/2 Diced Yellow Onion

Pita Bread

1/2 teaspoon of Fine Salt

1/4 teaspoon of Ground Black Pepper

Directions:

1. Whisk your eggs, salt, pepper, and milk in your large-sized bowl. Set to the side.

2. Heat your oil in your skillet over a medium heat until simmering. Add your onion. Stir occasionally, cook for approximately 5 minutes. Add your spinach, tossing until completely wilted and no liquid is left. Should take approximately 3 minutes.

3. Reduce your heat to a medium-low and pour in your egg mixture. Cook for approximately 2 minutes. Using your rubber spatula, push your set eggs from the edge of your skillet to the center. Spread your uncooked eggs back into an even layer. Repeat, pushing your set eggs from the edges to the center every 30 seconds until they are all nearly set. Total cooking time should be approximately 6 minutes.

4. Remove skillet from your heat and fold in your tomatoes. Toast your pita bread.

5. Serve!

Greek Frittata w/ Zucchini, Tomatoes, Feta, and Herbs (Serves 4)

Ingredients:

15 ounces of Diced Tomatoes

6 Eggs

1/2 cup of Mozzarella Cheese

1 Diced Medium Zucchini

1 tablespoon of Olive Oil

1/4 cup of Crumbled Feta Cheese

2 cloves of Minced Garlic

1/2 teaspoon of Dried Basil

1 tablespoon of Cream

1 teaspoon of Spike Seasoning

1/4 teaspoon of Oregano

Cracked Black Pepper

Directions:

1. Pour your tomatoes into your colander and allow them to drain out any liquid into your sink. Cut the ends off your zucchini and dice it into smaller pieces.

2. Preheat your broiler. Spray your frying pan with cooking spray. Heat your olive oil in your pan. Add your garlic, zucchini, spike seasoning, and dried herb. Saute them for approximately 3 minutes. Add your tomatoes and cook an additional 3 to 5 minutes. All your liquid from your tomatoes should be evaporated.

3. While your vegetables are cooking, break your eggs in your bowl and beat them well. Pour your eggs into your pan with your vegetable mix and cook an additional 2 to 3 minutes. Eggs should just be beginning to set.

4. Add half of your feta and mozzarella cheese. Stir them in gently. Cook for approximately 3 minutes. Sprinkle the rest of your feta and mozzarella cheese over top and allow to cook for 3 more minutes with a lid covering your pan. Cheese should be mostly melted and your eggs should be nearly set.

5. Place under your broiler until the top becomes browned slightly. Should only take a few minutes. Keep a close eye on it. Rotate the pan if necessary to get an even browning.

6. Sprinkle any additional fresh herbs if you so desire. Cut into pie shaped wedges.

7. Serve!

Mediterranean Omelet (Serves 4)

<u>Ingredients:</u>

2 Large Eggs

4 1/4 tablespoons of Feta Cheese

1 teaspoon of Olive Oil

1/2 teaspoon of Dried Oregano

1 Tomato

3 sprigs of Chives

Olives

Pinch of Salt

Directions:

1. In your frying pan heat your olive oil.

2. Add your chopped tomato, oregano, and onion. Cook until your tomatoes are no longer soft.

3. Add in your olives and turn off the heat. Add your feta cheese.

4. In a different frying pan add your eggs and salt and cook.

5. Combine your ingredients and add your toppings.

6. Serve!

Bananas Foster French Toast (Serves 6)

Ingredients:

French Toast:

2 Eggs

6 slices of Challah Bread

1 teaspoon of Vanilla Extract

1/2 cup of Milk

3 tablespoons of Granulated Sugar

1/2 teaspoon of Ground Cinnamon

Pinch of Salt

Butter (For Frying)

Banana Caramel Syrup:

1/4 cup of Butter

3 tablespoons of Heavy Whipping Cream

3/4 cup of Brown Sugar (Lightly Packed)

1 teaspoon of Vanilla Extract

1/4 teaspoon of Ground Cinnamon

2 Bananas (Thickly Sliced)

4 tablespoons of Dark Rum (Optional)

Directions:

1. In your bowl, whisk together your eggs, milk, vanilla, sugar, cinnamon, and salt. Set to the side.

2. Heat your frying pan over a medium-high heat. Add your pat of butter to your pan to melt.

3. Dip each slice of bread into your egg mixture until your bread has soaked up some of the liquid. Flip your bread and repeat on the other side. Add your soaked bread to your frying pan. Fry for approximately 2 to 3 minutes per side, depending on the thickness of your bread, until golden brown.

4. In your pot, melt your butter over a medium-high heat. Add your brown sugar and whisk gently to combine. Once your butter and sugar are incorporated together, stop whisking and let your mixture come to a low boil. Without stirring, let your sugar mixture boil for 2 minutes.

5. Slowly add your whipping cream and whisk to combine. Stir in your cinnamon and vanilla. Add your rum and banana slices. Cook for around 45 seconds to 1 minute or until your bananas begin to soften, but you don't want them to turn mushy.

6. Spoon your bananas and caramel syrup directly over your French toast.

7. Serve!

Spanish Omelette (Serves 4)

Ingredients:

4 Eggs

1 Large Thinly Sliced Potato

1 1/2 tablespoons of Butter

1 cup of Finely Chopped Onion

1/8 teaspoon of Ground Black Pepper

1/4 cup of Water

Pinch of Achiote Powder

Directions:

1. Melt your butter in your 12-inch skillet over a medium-high heat. Cook your potato, achiote, and onion. Stir it occasionally until your vegetables are tender and crisp. Should take approximately 5 minutes. Reduce your heat to a medium-low and cook until golden brown. Should take approximately 10 minutes.

2. Beat your eggs, pepper, and water with your whisk. Add your egg mix to your skillet and cook for approximately 6 minutes over a medium-low heat. Do not stir. Reduce your heat to low, cover, and continue to cook until your eggs are set. Should take about 4 minutes.

3. Carefully invert onto a large-sized plate and slide it back into your skillet. Cook for another 5 minutes until golden.

4. Serve!

Huevos Revueltos (Serves 4)

Ingredients:

4 Eggs

1/4 cup of Crumbled Queso Fresco Cheese

1/2 cup of Chopped Onion

2 tablespoons of Butter Spread

1/2 cup of Chopped Tomatoes

Chopped Fresh Cilantro

Directions:

1. Melt your butter spread in your skillet over a medium heat and add your vegetables. Stir occasionally, approximately 4 minutes or until they are tender. Add in your eggs. Stir frequently, approximately 2 minutes until your eggs are done.

2. Sprinkle with your cilantro and cheese.

3. Serve!

Waffled Falafel (Serves 4)

Ingredients:

2 Large Egg Whites

2 cans of Garbanzo Beans

1 1/2 tablespoons of All Purpose Flour

1/4 cup of Chopped Fresh Parsley

1 Chopped Medium Onion

1/4 cup of Chopped Fresh Cilantro

3 Cloves of Roasted Garlic

1/4 teaspoon of Cayenne Pepper

2 teaspoons of Ground Cumin

1 teaspoon of Ground Coriander

1/4 teaspoon of Ground Black Pepper

1 3/4 teaspoons of Salt

Pinch of Ground Cardamom

Cooking Spray

Directions:

1. Preheat your waffle iron. Spray inside of your iron with your cooking spray.

2. Process your garbanzo beans in your food processor until they are coarsely chopped.

3. Add in your egg whites, cilantro, onion, parsley, cumin, flour, coriander, garlic, salt, black pepper, cayenne pepper, and ground cardamom to your garbanzo beans.

4. Pulse in your food processor until your batter resembles a coarse meal. Scrap down the sides while pulsing.

5. Pour your batter into your bowl and stir it with your fork.

6. Spoon 1/4 cup of batter onto each section of your waffle iron. Cook until they are evenly browned. Should take approximately 5 minutes. Repeat the process with your batter until it has all been used.

7. Serve!

Creamy Cuban Fu Fu (Serves 8)

Ingredients:

1 Small Chopped Onion

4 slices of Chopped Bacon

1 clove of Chopped Garlic

4 Sliced Sweet Plantains

1/2 cup of Light Mayonnaise

Directions:

1. Cover your plantains with water in your 4-quart sauce pot. Bring your pot to a boil over a medium-high heat. Reduce your heat and allow it to simmer for approximately 10 minutes until your plantains are tender. Drain the water from your pot and mash your plantains. Set to the side.

2. Cook your bacon in your 10-inch skillet over a medium heat until your bacon is crisp. Drain the excess liquid. Reserve a tablespoon of your bacon drippings.

3. Heat your reserved drippings in the same skillet and cook your onion for approximately 4 minutes. Make sure to occasionally stir. Once your onion is tender, add your garlic and cook approximately 1 more minute.

4. Combine your plantains, onion mixture, 1/2 of the bacon, and mayonnaise in your serving bowl. Garnish it with your remaining bacon.

5. Serve!

Spanish Tortilla (Serves 6)

Ingredients:

6 Large Eggs

1 cup of Diced Cooked Red Potatoes

4 Large Egg Whites

1/2 cup of Shredded Jack or Manchego Cheese

1 Small Thinly Sliced Onion

1/2 teaspoon of Smoked Paprika

3 cups of Chopped Baby Spinach

1 tablespoon of Chopped Fresh Thyme

3 teaspoons of Extra-Virgin Olive Oil

1/2 teaspoon of Salt

1/2 teaspoon of Freshly Ground Pepper

Directions:

1. Heat 2 teaspoons of your oil in your medium skillet over a medium heat. Add your onion and cook, stirring until they become translucent. Add in your potatoes, paprika, and thyme. Cook for about 2 more minutes.

2. Lightly whisk your egg whites and eggs in your large-sized bowl. Gently stir your potato mixture into your eggs along with your spinach, cheese, pepper, and salt until well combined. Wipe your pan clean, add in your remaining oil and heat it over a medium heat. Pour in your egg mix. Cover and cook until your edges have set and the bottom is browned. Should take approximately 4 to 5 minutes.

3. Flip your tortilla and run your spatula around your edges to get them loosened. Invert a large-sized pan over your pan and turn your tortilla onto it. Slide your tortilla back into your original pan and cook until completely set in the middle. Should take around 3 to 6 minutes.

4. Serve!

Mediterranean Tofu Scramble (Serves 4)

Ingredients:

1 pound of Extra Firm Tofu

2 tablespoons of Olive Oil

3 Chopped Scallions

1 Diced Purple Onion

2 tablespoons of Soy Sauce

1 Diced Medium Red Bell Pepper

1 tablespoon of Lemon Juice

1 teaspoon of Ground Turmeric

1/4 cup of Finely Chopped Fresh Parsley

2 cloves of Minced Garlic

1/2 teaspoon of Red Pepper Flakes

2 tablespoons of Seasoning

Hummus

Toast

Pita Bread

Hot Sauce

Directions:

1. Coat the bottom of your large-sized skillet with your olive oil and put it over a medium heat. Once your oil is hot, add your onion and saute until it has softened. Should take around 5 minutes. Add your garlic and cook an additional minute.

2. Crumble your tofu into your skillet and add your soy sauce, bell pepper, seasoning, lemon juice, and red pepper flakes. Keep cooking, flipping with your spatula, until your bell pepper pieces are crisp and tender. Should take around 5 minutes. Remove from the heat and fold in your scallions and parsley.

3. Add your hummus, toast, pita bread, and hot sauce on the side.

4. Serve!

Totally Loaded Tuna Pasta Salad (Serves 4)

Ingredients:

12 ounces of Noodles

2/3 cup of Mayonnaise

3 Hard-Boiled Eggs

10 Whole Black Olives

1/4 cup of Diced Onions

1/2 cup of Diced Celery

2 Dill Pickles

1 can of Albacore

2 teaspoons of Pickle Juice

2 tablespoons of Bacon

Directions:

1. Boil your noodles and drain once cooked. You want them to be slightly al dente. Run some cool water over your noodles to help them cool down.

2. Dice your hard boiled eggs, pickles, olives, and flake your tuna.

3. Add your ingredients to your noodles and toss gently.

4. Add your mayonnaise and fold into your tuna pasta mix.

5. Add your pickle juice. Refrigerate for 2 hours.

6. Serve!

Roasted Asparagus Prosciutto & Egg (Serves 4)

Ingredients:

4 Eggs

1 bunch of Trimmed Fresh Asparagus

2 ounces of Minced Prosciutto

1 teaspoon of Distilled White Vinegar

1 tablespoon of Extra-Virgin Olive Oil

1 tablespoon of Olive Oil

1/2 of a Lemon (Juiced & Zested)

Pinch of Salt

Pinch of Ground Black Pepper

Directions:

1. Preheat your oven to 425 degrees.

2. Place your asparagus in your baking dish and then drizzle with your extra-virgin olive oil.

3. Heat your olive oil in your skillet over a medium-low heat. Add in your prosciutto. Cook approximately 3 to 4 minutes. Stir it until it is golden colored and rendered. Sprinkle your oil and prosciutto over your asparagus. Season with your pepper and toss it together to coat well.

4. Roast it in your oven for approximately 10 minutes. Take out and toss it again.

5. Place it back in your oven for an additional 5 minutes until your asparagus is firm yet still tender.

6. Fill your large-sized saucepan with approximately 2 to 3-inches of water and boil over a high heat. Reduce your heat to medium-low. Pour in your vinegar and salt.

7. Crack an egg into your bowl and then slip your egg gently into the water. Continue this with all of your remaining eggs. Poach your eggs until the whites are firm and the yolks have gotten thick but not hard. Should take approximately 4 to 6 minutes.

8. Remove your eggs using a slotted spoon. Dab on a towel to help remove any excess water. Move to a warm plate.

9. Drizzle lemon juice over your asparagus. Place your asparagus on plate and top it with your poached egg and a pinch of the lemon zest. Season it with your black pepper.

10. Serve!

Creamy Oatmeal Bowls w/ Raspberries, Seeds, & Honey (Serves 3)

Ingredients:

1 cup Rolled Oats

2 teaspoons of Butter

1/2 teaspoon of Ground Cinnamon

2 cups of Boiling Water

Pinch of Salt

Toppings:

Seeds / Nuts (Your Choice)

Fresh Berries / Fruit (Your Choice)

Honey

Directions:

1. Combine your oats, water, and salt in your saucepan then bring to a boil. Allow it to cook for approximately 5 minutes.

2. Turn down your heat and allow it to simmer for about 5 to 10 minutes, stirring regularly, until your oats are creamy and your water has been absorbed.

3. Take your pot off the heat. Add your butter and cinnamon then cover with a lid. Allow it to steam for approximately 5 minutes.

4. After 5 minutes, give your oats another stir then top with your nuts, berries, seeds, and a drizzle of honey.

5. Serve!

Creamy Loaded Mashed Potatoes (Serves 8)

<u>Ingredients:</u>

3 pounds of Cubed and Peeled Potatoes

6 slices of Bacon or Turkey Bacon

1 cup of Sour Cream

1 1/2 cups of Shredded Cheddar Cheese

1 cup of Mayonnaise

3 Chopped Green Onions

<u>Directions:</u>

1. Cover your potatoes with your water in a 4-quart sauce pot. Boil over a high heat. Reduce your heat to low and cook for approximately 10 minutes until your potatoes are tender. Drain them and mash.

2. Preheat your oven to 375 degrees. Spray your baking dish with your cooking spray.

3. Stir in your mayonnaise, green onions, 4 strips of crumbled bacon, and sour cream. Turn them into your baking dish and cook for approximately 30 minutes.

4. Top with your remaining 1/2 cup of cheese and your bacon. Bake for 5 more minutes until your cheese has melted.

5. Serve!

Greek Yogurt w/ Berries & Seeds (Serves 1)

Ingredients:

1 tablespoon of Greek Yogurt

1 handful of Blueberries

1 teaspoon of Pumpkin Seeds

1 handful of Raspberries

1 teaspoon of Sliced Almonds

1 teaspoon of Sunflower Seeds

Directions:

1. Wash and dry your berries. Place them into your dish.

2. Spoon your Greek yogurt on top and sprinkle with your seeds and nuts.

3. Serve!

Secret Breakfast Sundaes (Serves 4)

Ingredients:

6 slices of Bacon

5 tablespoons of Pure Maple Syrup or Pancake Syrup

1/2 cup of Heavy Whipping Cream

2 cups of Coffee Ice Cream

3/4 cup of Granola Cereal

2 cups of Butter Pecan Ice Cream

3 tablespoons of Light Brown Sugar

4 Fresh Strawberries

Directions:

1. Preheat your oven to 400 degrees.

2. Arrange your bacon on your non-stick baking sheet. Sprinkle 1/2 of your brown sugar over your bacon. Bake for approximately 6 minutes. Turn your bacon and sprinkle your remaining brown sugar over it. Bake for an additional 6 minutes until your bacon is dark brown. Remove from your oven and allow it to cool on your wire rack. Once your bacon has cooled, crumble it up and set it to the side.

3. Beat together a tablespoon of your maple syrup with a 1/2 cup of cream in your 2-quart metal bowl using an electric mixer. Beat until stiff peaks form and then set to the side.

4. Spoon 2 tablespoons of your granola into 4 parfait glasses. Evenly scoop your butter pecan ice cream into glasses and sprinkle them with your remaining granola. Add your coffee ice cream to each glass and evenly drizzle the remaining maple syrup on top. Sprinkle with your bacon, and top with your strawberries.

5. Serve!

Mediterranean Feta Egg Scramble (Serves 4)

Ingredients:

6 Eggs

3/4 cup of Crumbled Feta Cheese

2 tablespoons of Minced Green Onions

1/4 cup of Light Sour Cream

2 tablespoons of Diced Roasted Red Peppers

1/2 teaspoon of Basil

1/2 teaspoon of Oregano

1/4 teaspoon of Garlic Powder

Ground Black Pepper

1/4 teaspoon of Kosher Salt

Flour Tortillas or Crepes (optional)

Directions:

1. Preheat your skillet over a medium heat.

2. Whisk your eggs, salt, pepper, oregano, garlic powder, and sour cream until combined. Add in your feta cheese. Once your skillet is hot add a teaspoon of butter and add your egg mixture. Allow your eggs to begin to set before scraping the bottom of your pan to allow the liquid parts a chance to cook.

3. Stir in your green onions and roasted red peppers. Cook your eggs until they reach your desired preference.

4. Serve!

Green Eggs & Ham Scramble Mediterranean Style (Serves 3)

Ingredients:

8 Large Eggs

1/4 cup of Crumbled Feta Cheese

2 tablespoons of Milk

3 cups of Roasted Red Potatoes

3 tablespoons of Chopped Roasted Red Peppers

1 tablespoon of Extra-Virgin Olive Oil

1/4 cup of Chopped and Pitted Kalamata

8 strips of Cooked and Crumbled Bacon

3 tablespoons of Chopped Roasted Red Peppers

2 cups of Baby Spinach Leaves

1/4 teaspoon of Ground Black Pepper

1/2 teaspoon of Kosher Salt

Vegetable Broth

Paprika

Garlic Salt

Directions:

1. Preheat your oven to 375 degrees. Wash and quarter your red potatoes. Place in your mixing bowl. Pour in vegetable broth to cover them. Season with your garlic salt, pepper, and paprika. Stir your potatoes and place on your baking sheet. Cook for approximately 30 minutes until tender.

2. Heat your olive oil in your skillet over a medium heat. Once hot, add your spinach leaves. Cook until wilted. Remove from the heat and set to the side.

3. In your mixing bowl, place your milk, eggs, kosher salt, and ground black pepper. Whisk to combine them and pour into your large-sized skillet over a medium heat that's been sprayed with cooking spray. Stir your eggs until they are scrambled. Don't overcook your eggs. Add your roasted red peppers, bacon, spinach, kalamata, and feta cheese. Stir well to combine.

4. Place your roasted potatoes into your serving bowls and top with your scrambled eggs.

5. Serve!

Greek Yogurt Parfait (Serves 4)

Ingredients:

4 teaspoons of Honey

28 Clementine Segments

3 cups of Plain Fat-Free Greek Yogurt

1/4 cup of Shelled Unsalted Dry Roasted Chopped Pistachios

1 teaspoon of Vanilla Extract

Directions:

1. Combine your Greek yogurt and vanilla in your bowl. Spoon in 1/3 cup of your yogurt mixture into 4 parfait glasses. Top each of them with 1/2 teaspoon of honey, 1/2 tablespoon of nuts, and 5 clementine sections.

2. Top your parfaits with your remaining yogurt mixture. Top each with 1/2 teaspoon of honey, 1/2 tablespoon of nuts, and 2 clementine segments.

3. Serve!

Banana Nut Oatmeal (Serves 1)

Ingredients:

1 Peeled Banana

1/4 cup of Quick Cooking Oats

1 teaspoon of Flax Seeds

1/2 cup of Skim Milk

2 tablespoons of Chopped Walnuts

3 tablespoons of Honey

Directions:

1. Combine your milk, oats, walnuts, flax seeds, honey, and banana in your microwave safe bowl. Cook in your microwave for approximately 2 minutes on high.

2. Mash your banana using a fork and stir it into your mixture.

3. Serve!

Apricot Marmalade

Ingredients:

6.5 pounds of Firm Apricots

5 pounds of Sugar

1 glass of Water

1 glass of Lemon Juice

Directions:

1. Wash your apricots and remove their pits.

2. Place them in layers in your pot, alternating a layer of your apricots, a layer of sugar, a layer of apricots, a layer of sugar etc. Pour water on top.

3. Place your pot over a low heat and stir until all your sugar has dissolved.

4. Adjust heat to simmer your marmalade.

5. Stir constantly using a wooden ladle so your marmalade doesn't stick to your pot.

6. Cook your mixture until it gets shiny and transparent.

7. Once your marmalade is thick, add your lemon juice and allow it to boil.

8. Move off your burner and allow it to cool. Place it in your jars. Seal your jars to preserve your marmalade.

9. Serve!

Strawberry Marmalade

Ingredients:

1 1/4 pounds of Sugar

2 1/4 pounds of Strawberries.

Directions:

1. Wash your strawberries. Cut into smaller-sized pieces.

2. Put your strawberries in your casserole dish and cover them in sugar.

3. Allow them to sit overnight in order to get your juices extracted. This will turn your sugar into a red colored syrup.

4. Put your casserole dish on a high heat and stir constantly until your sugar has dissolved and fruit has boiled.

5. When it begins to foam, clean it using a spoon.

6. Lower the heat and stir often for approximately 20 minutes. You don't want your marmalade sticking to the bottom.

7. Take off the heat when it is shiny and thick.

8. Seal in your jars in order to preserve.

9. Serve!

Greek Yogurt Pancakes (Serves 6)

Ingredients:

1 cup of Old-Fashioned Oats

1/2 cup of All Purpose Flour

2 Large Eggs

2 tablespoons of Flax Seeds

1 teaspoon of Baking Soda

2 cups of Vanilla Greek Yogurt

2 tablespoons of Canola Oil

2 tablespoons of Honey or Agave

1/4 teaspoon of Salt

Fresh Fruit

Syrup

Directions:

1. Combine your oats, seeds, baking soda, flour, and salt in your blender and pulse for approximately 30 seconds.

2. Add in your eggs, yogurt, agave, and oil. Blend until it is smooth. Allow your batter to stand for approximately 20 minutes in order to thicken.

3. Heat your skillet over a medium heat. Brush your skillet with oil. Ladle your batter 1/4 of a cup at a time into your skillet. Cook your pancakes until the bottoms turn golden brown and bubbles begin forming on top. Should take about 2 minutes. Turn over your pancakes and cook until the bottoms are golden brown. Should take another 2 minutes.

4. Transfer your pancakes to your baking sheet. Keep warm in your oven. Repeat the process until all your batter is cooked.

5. Add on your desired amount of syrup and fruit toppings.

6. Serve!

Chapter Two: Mediterranean Diet Lunch Recipes

In this section, I will give you 25+ Mediterranean lunch recipes you can make yourself. I'll include both a few basic recipes and a few more advanced recipes. That way no matter what your level in the kitchen you'll be able to prepare yourself a heart-healthy Mediterranean meal to keep you on track with your diet.

Grilled Salmon & Zucchini w/ Red Pepper Sauce (Serves 4)

Ingredients:

1 1/4 pounds of Skinned Salmon Fillet (Cut Into 4 Portions)

1/4 cup of Chopped Jarred Roasted Red Peppers

1/4 cup of Halved Grape Tomatoes

2 Medium Zucchini

1/3 cup of Toasted Sliced Almonds

1 tablespoon of Sherry Vinegar

1 clove of Garlic

1 teaspoon of Paprika

1 tablespoon of Extra-Virgin Olive Oil

1 tablespoon of Chopped Fresh Parsley

3/4 teaspoon of Salt

1/2 teaspoon of Ground Pepper

Canola Cooking Spray

Directions:

1. Preheat your grill to a medium heat.

2. Process your peppers, almonds, garlic, vinegar, tomatoes, 1/4 teaspoon of salt, oil, paprika, and 1/4 teaspoon of pepper in your food processor until it is smooth. Set to the side.

3. Coat your zucchini and salmon on both sides with your cooking spray, then sprinkle with your remaining 1/2 teaspoon of salt and 1/4 teaspoon of pepper. Grill, turning it once until your salmon is cooked through and your zucchini has softened and turned brown. Should take approximately 3 minutes per side.

4. Transfer to a clean cutting board. Once cooled, slice into 1/2-inch pieces. Toss in your bowl with half of the sauce you set to the side earlier. Divide among 4 plates with a piece of salmon topped with your remaining 1/2 of your sauce. Garnish with parsley.

5. Serve!

Caprese Style Portobello (Serves)

Ingredients:

Large Portobello Mushroom Caps (Gills Removed)

Shredded or Fresh Mozzarella

Cherry Tomatoes (Halved)

Olive Oil

Fresh Basil

Directions:

1. Heat your oven to 400 degrees.

2. Line your baking sheet with foil.

3. Brush your caps and rims with your olive oil on each mushroom.

4. Slice your cherry or grape tomatoes in half, place in your bowl, drizzle with olive oil, add chopped basil, salt, and pepper. Allow it to sit for a few minutes to let your flavors meld.

5. Place your cheese on the bottom of your mushroom cap, spoon on your tomato basil mixture and bake until your cheese melts and the mushrooms are cooked but not overcooked.

6. Serve!

Fast Paella w/ Shrimp & Mussels (Serves 4)

Ingredients:

1 pound of Mussels

1 1/3 cups of Reduced-Sodium Chicken Broth

1 pound of Peeled Shrimp

2 cloves of Minced Garlic

1/2 cup of Chopped Onion

1/2 cup of Chopped Red Bell Pepper

2 cups of Instant Brown Rice

1 tablespoon of Extra-Virgin Olive Oil

1/2 teaspoon of Dried Thyme

1 cup of Frozen Peas (Thawed)

1/4 teaspoon of Ground Pepper

1/4 teaspoon of Salt

Pinch of Saffron

4 Lemon Wedges (Optional

Directions:

1. Heat your oil in your skillet over a medium heat. Add your bell pepper, garlic, and onion. Cook for approximately 3 minutes until your vegetables have softened. Be sure to stir occasionally. Add your broth, rice, saffron, pepper, and salt. Bring to a boil over a medium heat. Cover and continue to cook for approximately 5 minutes.

2. Stir in your peas and shrimp. Place your mussels on top of your rice in an even layer. Cover and cook for approximately 5 minutes until your mussels have opened and your rice is tender. Remove from the heat, still covered, allow to rest for another 5 minutes until your liquid is mostly absorbed. Add your lemon wedges to the side if you so desire.

3. Serve!

Seafood Linguine (Serves 4)

Ingredients:

28-ounce can of Diced Tomatoes

8 ounces of Whole-Wheat Linguine

2 tablespoons of Extra-Virgin Olive Oil

1 tablespoon of Chopped Fresh Marjoram

4 cloves of Chopped Garlic

1 tablespoon of Chopped Shallot

12 Small Cherrystone Clams (Scrubbed)

1/4 cup of Grated Parmesan Cheese

8 ounces of Tilapia (Cut Into 1-Inch Strips)

1/2 cup of White Wine

8 ounces of Dry Sea Scallops

1/4 teaspoon of Ground Pepper

1/2 teaspoon of Salt

Directions:

1. Bring your large-sized pot of water to a boil. Add your pasta and cook until tender. Should take approximately 8 to 10 minutes. Drain and rinse.

2. Heat your oil over a medium heat in your large-sized skillet. Add your shallot and garlic. Cook for about 1 minute, stirring until softened.

3. Increase your heat to a medium-high. Add your tomatoes, salt, wine, and pepper. Bring to a simmer, cooking for approximately 1 minute. Add your clams, cover, and cook for another 2 minutes. Stir in your fish, scallops, and marjoram. Cover and continue to cook until your fish and scallops are cooked through and your clams have opened. Should take approximately 3 to 5 minutes. Get rid of any clams that don't open up.

4. Spoon your sauce and your clams over the pasta. Sprinkle with your Parmesan cheese and additional marjoram.

5. Serve!

Tuna Pasta w/ Olives & Artichokes (Serves 4)

Ingredients:

8 ounces of Tuna Steak (Cut Into 3 Pieces)

1/4 cup of Chopped Fresh Basil

2 teaspoons of Freshly Grated Lemon Zest

2 cups of Grape Tomatoes

4 tablespoons of Extra-Virgin Olive Oil

6 ounces of Whole Wheat Penne Pasta

2 teaspoons of Chopped Fresh Rosemary

10-ounce package of Frozen Artichoke Hearts (Thawed)

3 cloves of Minced Garlic

2 tablespoons of Lemon Juice

1/2 cup of White Wine

1/4 cup of Chopped Green Olives

1/2 teaspoon of Salt

1/4 teaspoon of Ground Pepper

Directions:

1. Preheat your grill to a medium-high heat. Bring your large-sized pot of water to a boil.

2. Toss your 3 tuna pieces into your bowl with lemon zest, 1 tablespoon of fresh rosemary, 1 tablespoon of oil, 1/4 teaspoon of salt, and 1/4 teaspoon of pepper. Grill your tuna for about 3 minutes per side until cooked all the way through. Move to your plate. When cool enough to be handled, flake your tuna into small bite size pieces.

3. Cook your pasta according to the directions on the package. Drain once finished.

4. Heat your remaining 3 tablespoons of oil in your large-sized skillet over a medium heat. Add your olives, artichoke hearts, remaining rosemary, and garlic. Cook for about 3 to 4 minutes, stirring occasionally until your garlic begins to brown.

5. Add your wine and tomatoes. Bring to a boil and cook for approximately 3 minutes until your wine has reduced slightly and the tomatoes have broken down. Stir in your tuna pieces, pasta, lemon juice, and your remaining 1/4 teaspoon of salt. Cook for another 1 to 2 minutes until heated all the way through. Garnish with 1/4 cup of basil.

6. Serve!

Mediterranean Shrimp and Pasta (Serves 4)

Ingredients:

4 cups of Cooked Angel Hair Pasta

2 tablespoons of Drained Capers

1 pound of Peeled Medium Shrimp

1/4 cup of Crumbled Feta Cheese

2 cloves of Minced Garlic

2 cups of Chopped Tomato

2 teaspoons of Olive Oil

1/4 cup of Thinly Sliced Fresh Basil

1/3 cup of Chopped Pitted Kalamata Olives

1/4 teaspoon of Ground Black Pepper

Cooking spray

Directions:

1. Cook your pasta.

2. Heat your olive oil in your skillet coated with your cooking spray over a medium-high heat. Add your garlic and saute for about 30 seconds.

3. Add your shrimp and saute for 1 minute. Add your basil and tomato. Reduce the heat and simmer for approximately 3 minutes until your tomato is tender.

4. Stir in your capers, kalamata olives, and black pepper.

5. Combine your shrimp mixture and your pasta in your large-sized bowl. Toss it together well. Top with your cheese.

6. Serve!

Chicken Gyros & Tzatziki Sauce (Serves 4)

Ingredients:

4 Chicken Breasts (Pounded Into 1/2-Inch Thickness)

4 Pita

1 tablespoon of Mediterranean Seasoning

1/2 Thinly Sliced Red Onion

1 Thinly Sliced Red Pepper

Crumbled Feta Cheese (Optional)

Lettuce (Optional)

Tzatziki Sauce:

2 cups of Cold Plain Greek Yogurt

1/2 English cucumber (Peeled & Diced)

1/3 cup of Chopped Dill (Fresh or Frozen)

4 teaspoons of Minced Garlic

1 1/2 tablespoons of Freshly Squeezed Lemon Juice

1/2 teaspoon of Salt

Directions:

1. Puree all of your sauce ingredients in your blender or food processor. Cover and chill until ready to serve. (If you have time, make this a few hours in advance or the night before so that the flavors can marinate.)

2. Season your chicken breasts with your Mediterranean seasoning. Cook in your large-sized skillet over a medium heat for approximately 5 to 6 minutes on each side until cooked through. Cut into strips.

3. Lay your pitas on a clean surface. Add your lettuce chicken, red pepper strips, and onions. Top with your Tzatziki sauce and crumbled feta. Fold your pita over like a sandwich, or roll it into a tunnel shape.

4. Serve!

Eggplant Pomodoro Pasta (Serves 6)

Ingredients:

1 Medium Eggplant

4 teaspoons of Capers

2 tablespoons of Extra-Virgin Olive Oil

12 ounces of Whole Wheat Angel Hair Pasta

4 Diced Plum Tomatoes

2 tablespoons of Red Wine Vinegar

2 cloves of Minced Garlic

1/3 cup of Chopped Pitted Green Olives

1/4 cup of Chopped Fresh Parsley

1/4 teaspoon of Crushed Red Pepper

3/4 teaspoon of Salt

1/2 teaspoon of Ground Pepper

Directions:

1. Bring your pot of water to a boil.

2. Heat your oil over a medium heat. Add your eggplant and cook for approximately 5 minutes, stirring occasionally until softened. Add your garlic and cook for about 30 seconds to 1 minute until fragrant. Add your olives, tomatoes, capers, vinegar, pepper, crushed red pepper, and salt. Cook for around 5 to 7 minutes, stirring until your tomatoes start to break down.

3. Cook your pasta in boiling water for approximately 6 minutes until tender. Drain and divide your pasta among 6 separate bowls. Spoon your sauce over your pasta and sprinkle parsley on top.

4. Serve!

Mediterranean Seafood Grill w/ Skordalia (Serves 4)

Ingredients:

1 pound of Halibut Fillets (Quartered)

1/4 cup of Plain Greek Low-Fat Yogurt

1 pound of Yukon Gold Potatoes

8 cloves of Peeled Garlic

1 slice of Sourdough Bread w/ Crust Removed

1 Lemon (Zest & Juiced)

1/4 teaspoon of Dried Thyme

3 tablespoons of Olive Oil

2 Red Bell Peppers (Quartered)

1/2 Medium Sliced Red Onion

1 pound of Sliced Zucchini

1/2 teaspoon of Salt

Directions:

1. Peel your potatoes, and chop into 1-inch pieces. Place them in your large-sized pan, and cover them with cold water. Add your garlic, and cook it over a high heat for approximately 15 minutes or until your potatoes are easily pierced using a fork.

2. While your potatoes are cooking, tear your bread into 4 pieces and place them in your large-sized bowl. Spoon 2 to 3 tablespoons of cooking liquid from your potatoes over the bread. Stir this with your fork until smooth. Add your yogurt, 2 tablespoons of olive oil, and zest and juice of 1 lemon. Stir until a smooth paste begins to form.

3. Once your potatoes are done, place your large-sized bowl in your sink and set your colander on top of it. Drain your potatoes and garlic, reserving your cooking liquid. Transfer your potatoes to the bread mixture and mash until it's smooth. Add your reserved cooking liquid, 2 tablespoons at a time until your mixture takes the consistency of loose mashed potatoes. Stir in your salt and 2 teaspoons of olive oil. Cover and keep it warm until you're ready to serve.

4. Preheat your pan over a medium-high heat. Drizzle your fish with 1/2 teaspoon of olive oil and season with the remaining 1/2 teaspoon of salt and thyme. Cook your fish approximately 2 to 3 minutes on each side until your fish flakes when tested using a fork. Transfer to your plate. Cover and keep warm until you're ready to serve.

5. Place your bell pepper, red onion, and zucchini in your large-sized bowl. Drizzle with your remaining 1/2 teaspoon of olive oil. Toss until well coated. Arrange your bell pepper in your pan and cook for approximately 5 minutes over a medium heat. Add your zucchini and onion. Cook for about 10 minutes or until your vegetables become tender.

6. Serve!

Grilled Eggplant Parmesan Sandwich (Serves 4)

Ingredients:

1 Large Eggplant (Cut Into 12 Individual 1/4-Inch Thick Rounds)

4 Small Pieces of Foccacia Bread

1/2 cup of Shredded Part-Skim Mozzarella Cheese

1 cup of Crushed Fire Roasted Tomatoes

5 ounces of Baby Spinach

3 tablespoons of Finely Shredded Parmesan

3 tablespoons of Chopped Fresh Basil (Divided)

2 teaspoons of Extra-Virgin Olive Oil

1/4 teaspoon of Salt

Plastic Wrap

Canola Cooking Spray

Directions:

1. Preheat your grill to a medium-high heat.

2. Place your eggplant rounds on your baking sheet and sprinkle with salt. Lightly coat both sides with your cooking spray.

3. Combine your Parmesan and mozzarella together in your small sized bowl. Brush both sides of your bread with your olive oil.

4. Place your spinach in a microwave-safe bowl. Cover your bowl with plastic wrap and punch a few holes in the top of your wrap. Microwave your spinach on high until it has wilted. Should take approximately 2 to 3 minutes. Combine your tomatoes and 2 tablespoons of basil in your microwave-safe bowl. Cover and microwave until it is bubbling. Should take about 2 minutes.

5. Place all of your ingredients on your baking sheet with your eggplant rounds and place it on your grill. Grill for about 2 to 3 minutes on each side until your eggplant is soft and brown. Grill your bread for approximately 1 minute until toasted. Return your bread and eggplant to your baking sheet. Reduce your grill to a medium heat.

6. Place 1 eggplant round on top of every slice of bread. Layer 1 tablespoon of your tomatoes, 1 tablespoon of wilted spinach, and 1 tablespoon of your cheese on each slice of your eggplant. Repeat the process for all the pieces of eggplant. Sprinkle each one with a little bit of your remaining basil. Place back on your grill, close the lid on your grill and grill until your eggplant stack has gotten hot and your cheese has melted. Should take approximately 5 to 7 minutes.

7. Serve!

Spicy Seared Eggplant (Serves 4)

Ingredients:

2 Small Sliced Shallots

3 tablespoons of Sherry-Wine Vinegar

1 Medium Eggplant

2 tablespoons of Golden Raisins

4 Pitted Chopped Gaeta Olives

1 clove of Minced Garlic

1/4 teaspoon of Red Pepper Flakes

1 tablespoon of Sugar

1/4 cup + 4 teaspoons of Extra-Virgin Olive Oil

1 tablespoon of Capers

Vegetable Oil

Coarse Salt

Directions:

1. Slice your eggplant crosswise into 8 slices. Sprinkle your slices with salt. Place in your colander over your bowl. Allow it to stand for approximately 30 minutes. Rinse your eggplant and pat dry.

2. In your saucepan over a medium heat, combine your garlic, shallots, red pepper flakes, vinegar, sugar, and 3 tablespoons of water. Bring your mix to a boil. Cook for approximately 1 minute and remove from the heat. Stir in your raisins, olives, capers, and 1/4 cup of olive oil. Allow to cool to room temperature.

3. Heat your grill to high and brush the grates with your vegetable oil. Brush your eggplant with 4 teaspoons of olive oil. Cook your eggplant until it is tender and charred. Turn it over halfway through cooking at the 10-minute mark.

4. Arrange your eggplant on your platter and spoon your shallot mix over top. Cool to room temperature.

5. Serve!

Ginger Shrimp w/ Charred Tomato Relish (Serves 4)

Ingredients:

20 Peeled Extra-Large Shrimp (Tails Left On)

4 Ripe Plum Tomatoes (Halved)

2 cloves of Minced Garlic

1 1/2 tablespoons of Grated Peeled Ginger

3 tablespoons of Vegetable Oil

1 tablespoon of Minced Fresh Jalapeno Pepper w/ Seeds

2 Medium Green Tomatoes (Halved)

2 tablespoons of Fresh Lime Juice

1 tablespoon of Chopped Cilantro

1 teaspoon of Sugar

1 tablespoon of Chopped Basil

Ground Black Pepper

Coarse Salt

20 Skewers

Directions:

1. Soak 20 skewers in your pan of water for approximately 30 minutes.

2. Stir together your ginger and garlic in a medium-sized bowl. Transfer half of your mixture to a large-sized bowl and stir in 2 tablespoons of oil. Add your shrimp, toss until it is all evenly coated. Cover and place in your refrigerator for at least 30 minutes. Cover your remaining mixture and refrigerate.

3. Heat your grill to high and lightly oil your grates. In your medium-sized bowl toss your green and plum tomatoes with your remaining tablespoon of oil. Season it with your pepper and salt. Grill your tomatoes, cut side facing up until the skins are charred and the flesh itself is tender. It should take approximately 4 to 6 minutes for your plum tomatoes and about 8 to 10 minutes for your green tomatoes. Be careful while grilling your tomatoes. The juices can sometimes cause a flare-up on your grill.

4. Once your tomatoes have cooled enough to handle, remove the skins and discard both the skins and the seeds. Finely chop your tomatoes flesh and add to the bowl with your reserved garlic / ginger mixture. Add your lime juice, cilantro, jalapeno, sugar, and basil.

5. Season your shrimp with pepper and salt. Thread the shrimp, lengthwise, onto your skewers, going through the tail and top of your shrimp. There is only one shrimp per skewer. Grill your shrimp until they are opaque. This should take about 2 minutes on each side.

6. Place your shrimp on your platter with a bowl of your relish.

7. Serve!

Penne w/ Vodka Sauce & Capicola (Serves 6)

Ingredients:

28 ounce can of Crushed Tomatoes

1/2 cup of Vodka

12 ounces of Whole Wheat Penne

2-ounce piece of Finely Diced Capicola or Pancetta

1/4 teaspoon of Crushed Red Pepper

1 Small Chopped Onion

1/4 cup of Chopped Fresh Basil

1/4 cup of Half and Half

3 cloves of Chopped Garlic

2 teaspoons of Worcestershire Sauce

Ground Pepper

Directions:

1. Bring your large-sized pot of water to a boil. Cook your penne for approximately 12 minutes until tender.

2. Cook your capicola or pancetta in your large-sized saucepan over a medium heat until it is crisp. Should take approximately 4 minutes. Drain it on your paper towel.

3. Return your saucepan to a medium-low heat. Add your garlic and onion. Cook for approximately 1 minute until your onion is translucent. Increase the heat to high and add in your vodka, bringing it to a boil. Continue to boil until reduced by about half. Should take about 2 minutes. Stir in your half and half, tomatoes, Worcestershire sauce, and red pepper. Reduce to a simmer and continue to cook for approximately 10 minutes until thickened.

4. Drain your pasta and add your sauce. Sprinkle some basil, pepper, and capicola or pancetta on top.

5. Serve!

Mediterranean Pizza (Serves 4)

Ingredients:

1 Prepared 12-inch Pizza Crust

1 cup of Crumbled Goat Cheese

3 Sliced Plum Tomatoes

1/4 teaspoon of Dried Italian Seasoning

14 ounces of Quartered Artichoke Hearts

1/4 teaspoon of Crushed Red Pepper

1/4 cup of Chopped Fresh Basil

6 Chopped Pitted Kalamata Olives

Cooking Spray

Directions:

1. Preheat your oven to 450 degrees.

2. Sprinkle your pizza crust with dried Italian seasoning and crushed red pepper.

3. Evenly sprinkle the crumbled goat cheese on your crust, leaving yourself a 1/2-inch border. Use the back of your spoon to press the cheese gently down on your pizza crust.

4. Arrange your chopped olives, plum tomato slices, and artichoke hearts on your pizza.

5. Place your pizza on your baking sheet coated with your cooking spray. Bake your pizza for about 10 to 12 minutes or until your crust is crisp and your cheese is bubbly.

6. Sprinkle your chopped basil over your pizza.

7. Serve!

Bean Bolognese (Serves 4)

Ingredients:

14 ounces of Salad Beans

1/2 cup of Chopped Carrot

1 Small Chopped Onion

1/4 cup of Chopped Celery

2 tablespoons of Extra-Virgin Olive Oil

1/2 cup of White Wine

1/2 cup of Grated Parmesan Cheese

8 ounces of Whole Wheat Fettuccine

4 cloves of Chopped Garlic

14 ounces of Diced Tomatoes

1/4 cup of Chopped Fresh Parsley

1 Bay Leaf

1/2 teaspoon of Salt

Directions:

1. Bring your large-sized pot of water to a boil. Mash 1/2 cup of your beans in your bowl using a fork.

2. Heat your oil in a medium-sized saucepan over a medium heat. Add your celery, onion, salt, and carrot. Cover and cook for approximately 10 minutes, stirring occasionally until it has softened. Add your bay leaf and garlic. Cook about 15 seconds until fragrant. Add your wine and turn the heat up to high and boil until the majority of your liquid has evaporated. Should take around 3 to 4 minutes.

3. Add your tomatoes and their juices, mashed beans, and 2 tablespoons of parsley. Bring to a simmer and stir occasionally until it has thickened. Should take approximately 6 minutes. Add your remaining whole beans. Cook for about 2 more minutes until heated through.

4. Cook your pasta in your boiling water. Should take approximately 9 minutes until tender. Drain it out into your colander.

5. Divide your pasta into 4 bowls. Discard your bay leaf and top your pasta with your sauce. Sprinkle parmesan and remaining parsley on top.

6. Serve!

Paprika Shrimp & Green Bean Saute (Serves 6)

Ingredients:

1 pound of Peeled & Deveined Raw Shrimp

4 cups of Trimmed Green Beans

2 16-ounce can of Large Butter Beans

3 tablespoons of Extra-Virgin Olive Oil

1/4 cup of Minced Garlic

2 teaspoons of Paprika

1/2 cup of Fresh Parsley

1/4 cup of Red Wine Vinegar

1/2 teaspoon of Salt

Ground Pepper

Directions:

1. Bring an inch of water to a boil in your large-sized saucepan. Put your green beans in your steamer basket and place in your pan. Cover and steam for approximately 4 to 6 minutes until tender-crisp.

2. Heat your oil over a medium-high heat in your large-sized skillet. Add your paprika and garlic, stirring constantly, for 20 seconds until fragrant but not yet browned. Add your shrimp and cook until they are opaque and pink. Should take about 2 minutes per side. Stir in your vinegar, beans, and salt. Cook for approximately 2 minutes until heated through. Stir in 1/4 cup of parsley.

3. Divide your green beans among 6 separate plates. Top with your shrimp mixture. Sprinkle with your ground pepper and your remaining 1/4 cup of parsley.

4. Serve!

Tortellini Primavera (Serves 5)

Ingredients:

4 cups of Chopped Vegetables (Carrots, Broccoli, Snap Peas)

14-ounce can of Vegetable Broth

16-ounce package of Frozen Cheese Tortellini

3 cloves of Sliced Garlic

1 cup of Shredded Fontina Cheese

1 tablespoon of Extra-Virgin Olive Oil

1 tablespoon of Chopped Fresh Tarragon

2 tablespoons of All-Purpose Flour

1/8 teaspoon of Salt

Directions:

1. Bring your large-sized pot of water to a boil.

2. Whisk together your flour and broth in your small-sized bowl. Heat your oil in your large-sized skillet over a medium heat. Add your garlic and cook for about 1 to 2 minutes, stirring frequently until your garlic begins to brown. Add your broth mix to the pan, bring it to a boil and cook for another 3 minutes until the sauce is thick. Remove from the heat and stir in your tarragon, salt, and cheese.

3. Add your tortellini and vegetables to the boiling water. Return the water to a simmer. Cook for approximately 3 to 5 minutes until the tortellini and vegetables are both tender. Drain the water from your pot and add to the pan containing your sauce. Stir to coat.

4. Serve!

Garlic & Vegetable Calzone (Serves 2)

Ingredients:

1/2 pound of Frozen Whole-Wheat Bread Dough (Thawed)

3 Asparagus Stalks (Cut In 1-Inch Pieces)

1/2 cup of Sliced Mushrooms

1/2 cup of Chopped Broccoli

1/2 cup of Shredded Mozzarella Cheese

1/2 cup of Chopped Spinach

2 teaspoons of Olive Oil

2/3 cup of Pizza Sauce

2 tablespoons of Minced Garlic

1 Medium Sliced Tomato

Directions:

1. Preheat your oven to 400 degrees. Lightly coat your baking sheet with cooking spray.

2. In your medium-sized bowl, add your spinach, asparagus, mushrooms, garlic, and broccoli. Drizzle 1 teaspoon of your olive oil over your vegetables and toss them together to mix.

3. Heat your large-sized frying pan over a medium-high heat. Add your vegetables and saute for approximately 4 to 5 minutes. Stir frequently. Remove from the heat and allow it to cool.

4. On a floured surface, cut your bread dough in half. Press each of your halves into a circle. Use your rolling pin and roll your dough into an oval shape. On one 1/2 of your oval, add 1/2 of your sauteed vegetables, 1/2 of your tomato slices, and 1/4 cup of your cheese. Wet your finger and rub the edge of your dough that has your filling on it. Fold your dough over the filling and press your edges together. Roll your edges and press down with a fork. Place your calzone on your baking sheet. Repeat the process to make the other calzone.

5. Brush your calzones with your remaining teaspoon of olive oil. Bake for approximately 20 minutes until golden brown.

6. Heat your pizza sauce in your microwave. Place each of your calzones on a plate. Each one gets a 1/3 cup of pizza sauce. You can place it on the side or pour it on top of the calzone.

7. Serve!

Shrimp Saltimbocca w/ Polenta (Serves 4)

Ingredients:

1 pound of Peeled & Deveined Raw Shrimp

18-ounce tube of Polenta (Cut Into 8 Rounds)

1/2 ounce of Thinly Sliced Prosciutto

2 tablespoons of Lemon Juice

1 1/4 teaspoons of Cornstarch

2 tablespoons of Finely Diced Onion

1 tablespoon of Extra-Virgin Olive Oil

3/4 cup of Clam Juice

1 tablespoon of Fresh Chopped Sage

1/4 teaspoon of Ground Pepper

Directions:

1. Position your rack in the center of your oven. Preheat your boiler. Coat your baking sheet with your cooking spray.

2. Place your prosciutto and polenta rounds on your baking sheet. Broil on the center rack for approximately 4 to 5 minutes until your prosciutto is crisp. Transfer your prosciutto to your plate. Continue to broil your polenta, turning once, until it becomes golden brown. Should take approximately 10 to 12 minutes per side.

3. Whisk your cornstarch and lemon juice in your small-sized bowl. Sprinkle your shrimp with 1/8 teaspoon of pepper. Heat your oil in your large-sized skillet over a medium heat. Add your onion and cook, stirring for about 2 to 3 minutes until beginning to brown. Add your shrimp and cook, stirring for another 2 minutes until your shrimp have turned pink but aren't cooked through. Pour in your clam juice, bring to a boil and cook until your liquid is reduced slightly. Should take approximately 2 minutes.

4. Whisk your cornstarch mixture again and add to your pan with the sage and the remaining 1/8 teaspoon of pepper. Cook, stirring until it has thickened. Should take approximately 1 to 2 minutes. Top your polenta with your shrimp and sauce. Crumble your prosciutto over top of it.

5. Serve!

Polenta w/ Roasted Mediterranean Vegetables (Serves 6)

Ingredients:

6 Medium Sliced Mushrooms

1 1/2 cups of Coarse Polenta (Corn Grits)

1 Small Yellow Zucchini (Cut Into 1/4-Inch Slices)

1 Small Green Zucchini (Cut Into 1/4-Inch Slices)

1 Small Peeled Eggplant (Cut Into 1/4-Inch Slices)

1 Seeded Sweet Red Pepper (Cut Into Chunks)

10 ounces of Frozen Spinach (Thawed)

2 Sliced Plum Roma Tomatoes

6 cups of Water

2 tablespoons + 1 teaspoon of Extra-Virgin Olive Oil

10 Chopped Ripe Olives

2 teaspoons of Trans-Free Margarine

6 Dry Packed Chopped Sun-Dried Tomatoes

2 teaspoons of Oregano

1/4 teaspoon of Cracked Black Pepper

Directions:

1. Heat your broiler. Position your rack approximately 4-inches from your heat source.

2. Brush your eggplant, mushrooms, zucchini, red pepper, and 1 tablespoon of olive oil. Arrange in 1 layer on your baking sheet and broil it under a low heat. Turn as is needed and occasionally brush with 1 tablespoon of olive oil. Once slightly browned and tender remove from your broiler.

3. Preheat your oven to 350 degrees. Coat your baking dish with your cooking spray.

4. In your medium-sized saucepan, bring your water to a boil. Reduce the heat and whisk in your polenta slowly. Continue to stir and cook approximately 5 minutes. Once your polenta comes away from the side of your pan, stir in your margarine and season with 1/8 teaspoon of black pepper. Remove from heat.

5. Spread your polenta into the sides and base of your baking dish. Brush with 1 teaspoon of olive oil. Place in your oven and bake for approximately 10 minutes. Remove from your oven and keep warm.

6. Drain your spinach and press it between your paper towels. Top your polenta with the spinach. Arrange a layer of your sliced tomatoes, olives, and chopped sun-dried tomatoes. Top with your remaining amount of roasted vegetables. Sprinkle with oregano and 1/8 teaspoon of black pepper.

7. Place back in your oven for approximately 10 minutes. Once warmed all the way through, remove from your oven. Cut into 6 wedges.

8. Serve!

Portobello Mushrooms w/ Mediterranean Stuffing (Serves 4)

Ingredients:

4 Portobello Caps

4 cups of Mixed Salad Greens

3 cups of Cubed Toasted French Bread

1/4 cup of Finely Chopped Onion

1/4 cup of Finely Chopped Red Bell Pepper

1/4 cup of Finely Chopped Celery

1/4 cup of Finely Chopped Green Bell Pepper

1/4 cup of Finely Chopped Carrot

1/4 teaspoon of Dried Italian Seasoning

1/2 cup of Crumbled Feta Cheese

1/4 teaspoon of Grated Parmesan Cheese

1/2 cup of Vegetable Broth

3 tablespoons of Low-Fat Balsamic Vinaigrette

2 cloves of Minced Garlic

1/4 teaspoon of Black Pepper

Cooking spray

Directions:

1. Preheat your oven to 350 degrees.

2. Remove the stems from your mushrooms and finely chop your stems. Measure out a 1/4 cup of stems and discard the rest. Combine your chopped stems, garlic, onions, carrot, celery, red pepper, green pepper, and dried Italian seasoning.

3. Heat your large-sized skillet over a medium heat and coat with your cooking spray. Add your onion mixture to the pan. Cook for approximately 10 minutes or until your vegetables have gotten tender. Combine your onion mixture and toasted French bread in your large-sized bowl. Toss them together to combine. Slowly add your vegetable broth, tossing to coat. Add your feta cheese and toss again to coat.

4. Remove the brown gills from underneath your mushroom caps using your spoon. Discard these gills. Place your mushrooms, stem sides up, on your baking sheet coated in cooking spray. Evenly brush your mushrooms with 1 tablespoon of vinaigrette. Sprinkle your black pepper and Parmesan cheese evenly over your mushrooms. Top each of your mushrooms with 1/2 cup of your bread mixture.

5. Bake in your oven for approximately 25 minutes until your mushrooms are tender.

6. Combine the remaining 2 tablespoons of your vinaigrette and greens. Toss gently to combine. Place 1 cup of your greens on each of the 4 serving plates. Top each bed of greens with 1 mushroom.

7. Serve!

Mediterranean Chicken Wrap (Serves 1)

Ingredients:

1 Chicken Cutlet

1/2 Small Thinly Sliced Tomato

10-Inch Whole Wheat Wrap

2 Thinly Sliced Dry Artichoke Hearts

1/4 cup of Mixed Baby Greens

1 tablespoon of Olive Tapenade

Pepper

Coarse Salt

Directions:

1. Cook your chicken.

2. Heat your broiler with your rack about 4-inches away from the heat. Season your chicken with salt and pepper. Broil for approximately 4 to 5 minutes until opaque. Allow it to cool.

3. Spread the bottom of your wrap with your olive tapenade. Layer your chicken, artichoke hearts, baby greens, and tomato. Season with your pepper and salt. Fold your tortilla to seal it.

4. Serve!

Stuffed Chicken Thighs Braised in Tomato Sauce (Serves 10)

Ingredients:

Chicken & Stuffing:

10 5-ounce Trimmed Boneless Skinless Chicken Thighs

1 Large Egg

1 cup of Fresh Whole Wheat Breadcrumbs

2 teaspoons of Chopped Thyme

4 ounces of Fresh Chopped Chicken Livers

1 cup of Frozen Cooked Spinach (Thawed)

1 tablespoon of Chopped Garlic

1/2 cup of Grated Parmesan Cheese

2 tablespoons of Finely Chopped Shallots

2 tablespoons of Extra-Virgin Olive Oil

1/2 teaspoon of Salt

3/4 teaspoon of Ground Pepper

Kitchen String

<u>Sauce:</u>

2 tablespoons of Minced Garlic

1 1/2 cups of Dry White Wine

1/2 cup of Finely Chopped Carrot

2 cups of Finely Chopped Onion

1/4 cup of Finely Chopped Shallot

28-ounce can of Crushed Tomatoes

1/2 cup of Diced Fennel Bulb

3 cups of Reduced-Sodium Chicken Broth

2 tablespoons of Chopped Fresh Basil

2 teaspoons of Chopped Fresh Thyme

1/2 teaspoon of Ground Pepper

1/4 teaspoon of Salt

Directions:

1. For your chicken & stuffing, combine your breadcrumbs and spinach in your medium-sized bowl. Add your chicken livers, egg, parmesan, 2 tablespoons of shallot, 1/2 teaspoon of pepper, 1/4 teaspoon of salt, and 1 tablespoon of garlic until well blended. Cover and refrigerate for a minimum of 30 minutes.

2. Place your chicken thighs with the skinned-side down on your work surface. Fill your thigh with 2 to 3 tablespoons of your stuffing, first filling the pocket left by the bone and then placing the rest in the center of the thigh. Roll your thigh closed and secure with 2 pieces of kitchen string. Repeat this process with all of the remaining thighs and stuffing. Season with your remaining 1/4 teaspoon of salt and pepper.

3. Heat your oil in your large-sized skillet over a medium-high heat. Reduce your heat to medium and add in half of your chicken thighs, seam side facing down. Cook for approximately 7 to 10 minutes, turning 2 or 3 times until the thighs are brown on every side. Transfer to an empty plate and continue this process with your remaining chicken thighs.

4. For your sauce, add your carrot, onion, fennel, 2 tablespoons of garlic, and 1/4 cup of shallot to your pan. Cover and cook for approximately 5 minutes until your vegetables are beginning to get browned and have become soft. Add your wine and scrape up any of the browned bits. Bring to a boil over a medium heat and continue boiling until your liquid is reduced by half. Should take around 6 to 8 minutes. Stir in your tomatoes, broth, thyme, basil, and chicken thighs.

5. Bring to a boil over a high heat and reduce your heat to a simmer. Cook this uncovered for approximately 35 to 40 minutes, turning your thighs occasionally until your thighs are tender and cooked through.

6. Remove your thighs using a slotted spoon. Tent with some foil to keep warm. Continue to simmer your sauce to further thicken it. Season with 1/4 teaspoon of salt and 1/2 teaspoon of pepper.

7. Serve!

Shrimp Panzanella (Serves 6)

Ingredients:

4 cups of 1/2-inch Multi-Grain Bread Cubes

1 pound of Chopped Peeled Cooked Shrimp

1/4 cup of Sliced Pitted Kalamata Olives + 1/4 cup of Olive Brine

4 tablespoons of Extra-Virgin Olive Oil

1 1/2 teaspoons of Chopped Fresh Thyme

4 Large Ripe Firm Chopped Tomatoes

1 clove of Peeled & Halved Garlic

1/4 cup of Chopped Fresh Chives

2 Large Red and Green Diced Bell Peppers

3/4 cup of Chopped Fresh Parsley

3 tablespoons of Red Wine Vinegar

4 cups of Mixed Salad Greens

Ground Pepper

Directions:

1. Preheat your oven to 350 degrees.

2. Drizzle 2 tablespoons of your oil on your baking sheet. Mash your garlic into your oil using a fork to help infuse it with flavor. Discard your garlic. Stir in your bread cubes until lightly coated in oil. Bake, stirring every 5 minutes, until very crisp. Should bake for approximately 12 to 15 minutes. Allow it to cool completely.

3. Combine your tomatoes, parsley, shrimp, bell peppers, olives, chives, olive brine, thyme, 2 remaining tablespoons of oil, and vinegar in a large-sized bowl. Season with your pepper. Allow it to stand for 10 minutes to blend the flavors.

4. Toss your croutons with your shrimp mixture and add over your mixed salad greens.

5. Serve!

Garlic Mushroom Kabobs (Serves 6)

Ingredients:

1/4 cup of Balsamic Vinegar

1 pound of Cremini Mushrooms

2 tablespoons Olive Oil

1/2 teaspoon of Dried Oregano

3 cloves of Pressed Garlic

2 tablespoons of Chopped Fresh Parsley Leaves

1/2 teaspoon of Dried Basil

Ground Black Pepper

Kosher Salt

Directions:

1. Preheat your oven to 425 degree. Lightly oil your baking sheet or coat with your nonstick spray.

2. In your large-sized bowl, whisk together your balsamic vinegar, garlic, olive oil, basil, and oregano. Season with your salt and pepper. Stir in your mushrooms and allow it to sit for approximately 10-15 minutes.

3. Thread your mushrooms onto your skewers and place them onto your prepared baking sheet. Place into your oven and roast until tender. Should take about 15 to 20 minutes.

4. Garnish with your parsley.

5. Serve!

Zucchini, Fennel & White Bean Pasta (Serves 4)

Ingredients:

2 Medium Zucchini

3/4 cup of Crumbled Hard Goat Cheese

1 Large Fennel Bulb (Trimmed)

1 cup of Cooked Cannellini Beans + 1/2 cup of Bean Cooking Liquid

6 tablespoons of Extra-Virgin Olive Oil

1/4 cup of Fresh Mint Leaves

4 cloves of Finely Chopped Garlic

8 ounces of Whole Wheat Penne

2 Diced Plum Tomatoes

1 Chopped Celery Stalk

1 Small Chopped Onion

1 1/4 teaspoons of Salt

Ground Pepper

Directions:

1. Place your beans in your large-sized bowl and cover with 3-inches of cold water. Soak for at least 4 hours.

2. Heat 3 tablespoons of your olive oil in your saucepan over a medium heat. Add your chopped onion, chopped celery stalk, and 2 chopped garlic cloves. Cook for approximately 3 to 4 minutes until the vegetables begin to soften. Drain your beans and add to your pan. Cover your beans by 1-inch with water. Bring to a boil and continue to boil for about 5 minutes. Lower the heat to a bare simmer, partially cover and cook 20 minutes to 3 hours until your beans are tender. Time will depend on the freshness of your beans. If your liquid level drops below the beans add 1 cup of hot water. Stir occasionally. Once your beans are soft, stir in 1 teaspoon of salt.

3. Preheat your oven to 400 degrees.

4. Cut your fennel bulb in half lengthwise and slice into 1/2-inch wedges. Quarter your zucchini lengthwise. Toss your zucchini and fennel with 1 tablespoon of your oil and salt. Arrange on your large-sized baking sheet in a single layer. Roast, turning it once, until soft and beginning to brown. Should take approximately 20 minutes.

5. Bring a large-sized pot of water to a boil. Add your pasta. Cook for about 8 to 10 minutes until your pasta is tender.

6. Heat your remaining 2 tablespoons of oil in your skillet over a medium heat. Add your remaining garlic and cook for approximately 30 seconds, stirring occasionally. Remove from the heat.

7. Once your vegetables have cooled down, chop them coarsely. Add your vegetables, beans, and the bean cooking liquid to your pan with the garlic and place over a medium-low heat. Drain your pasta and immediately add it to your pan. Toss it well and add your tomatoes. Continue to toss until warmed up. Remove from the heat and stir in your cheese and mint. Season with pepper.

8. Serve!

Mediterranean Wrap (Serves 4)

Ingredients:

1 pound of Chicken Tenders

1 cup of Chopped Cucumber

1 cup of Chopped Fresh Parsley

1/2 cup of Chopped Fresh Mint

1/3 cup of Whole Wheat Couscous

1/4 cup of Lemon Juice

2 teaspoons of Minced Garlic

3 tablespoons of Extra-Virgin Olive Oil

1 Medium Chopped Tomato

1/2 cup of Water

4 10-inch Spinach or Sun-Dried Tomato Wraps or Tortillas

1/4 teaspoon of Ground Pepper

1/4 teaspoon of Salt

Directions:

1. Bring your water to a boil in your small-sized saucepan. Stir in your couscous and remove it from the heat. Cover your saucepan and allow it to stand for approximately 5 minutes. Fluff it using a fork. Set to the side.

2. Combine your mint, parsley, oil, lemon juice, garlic, 1/8 teaspoon of salt, and a 1/8 teaspoon of pepper in your small-sized bowl.

3. Toss your chicken tenders in your medium bowl with a tablespoon of your parsley mixture and the remaining 1/8 teaspoon of salt. Place your tenders in your large-sized skillet and cook over a medium heat for approximately 3 to 5 minutes per side until cooked through. Transfer over to a clean cutting board. Once cool enough to handle, cut into bite-sized pieces.

4. Stir your remaining parsley mixture into your couscous along with your cucumber and tomato.

5. Assemble the wraps. Spread a 3/4 cup of couscous mixture onto each of your wraps. Divide your chicken evenly among the wraps. Roll your wraps up like a burrito, tucking in the sides to hold all the ingredients in. Cut each one in half.

6. Serve!

Chapter Three: Mediterranean Diet Dinner Recipes

In this section, I will give you 30+ Mediterranean dinner recipes you can make yourself. I'll include both a few basic recipes and a few more advanced recipes. That way no matter what your level in the kitchen you'll be able to prepare yourself a heart-healthy Mediterranean meal to keep you on track with your diet.

Mediterranean Grilled Vegetable Tagine (Serves 4)

Ingredients:

2 Quartered Red Bell Peppers

1 Small Red Onion

2 cloves of Minced Garlic

2 Quartered Green Bell Peppers

1 teaspoon of Olive Oil

1/4 teaspoon of Ground Cinnamon

1 3/4 cups of Chopped Onion

1 teaspoon of Ground Cumin

1/2 teaspoon of Crushed Fennel Seeds

1/4 cup of Sliced Pitted Green Olives

1/4 cup of Golden Raisins

1 1/4 cups of Water

2 teaspoons of Balsamic Vinegar

1 28-ounce can of Diced Tomatoes

6 Small Quartered Red Potatoes

1/4 cup of Toasted Pine Nuts

2/3 cup of Uncooked Couscous

1/2 teaspoon of Kosher Salt

1/4 teaspoon of Ground Black Pepper

Cooking Spray

Directions:

1. Cut your red onion into 4 wedges, leaving your root end still intact. Place your peppers, red onion, 1/4 teaspoon of salt, vinegar, and 1/2 teaspoon of oil in your zip-top plastic bag. Seal your bag and toss to coat well.

2. Heat a 1/2 teaspoon of oil over a medium-high heat in your large-sized skillet. Add your garlic and chopped onion. Saute for approximately 3 minutes. Add your fennel, cumin, and cinnamon. Saute for 1 minute. Add your olives, 1/4 cup of water, 1/4 teaspoon of salt, raisins, tomatoes, black pepper, and potatoes. Bring to a boil. Cover and reduce the heat. Allow to simmer for approximately 25 minutes until your potatoes are tender.

3. Remove your red onion and bell peppers from your bag. Discard the marinade. Place on your grill rack that's been coated with cooking spray. Grill for approximately 10 minutes, turning them frequently.

4. Bring a cup of water to a boil in your medium sized saucepan, gradually stirring in your couscous. Remove it from the heat and cover. Allow it to stand for approximately 5 minutes. Fluff using a fork. Add your tomato mixture over the couscous. Top with your grilled red onions and bell peppers. Sprinkle some pine nuts on top.

5. Serve!

Grilled Chicken & Dill Greek Yogurt Sauce (Serves 8)

Ingredients:

Grilled Chicken:

8 Boneless Skinless Chicken Thighs

10 Minced Garlic Cloves

1/2 teaspoon of Allspice

1/2 teaspoon of Paprika

1/4 teaspoon of Ground Green Cardamom

1/2 teaspoon of Ground Nutmeg

1 Medium Sliced Red Onion

5 tablespoons of Olive Oil

2 Lemons (Juiced)

Salt

Pepper

Dill Greek Yogurt Sauce:

1 Minced Garlic Clove

1 1/4 cup of Greek Yogurt

1 cup of Chopped Fresh Dill (Stems Removed)

1 tablespoon of Olive Oil

1/2 Lemon (Juiced)

Salt

Pinch of Cayenne Pepper (Optional)

Directions:

1. Combine your minced garlic, fresh dill, yogurt, olive oil, lemon juice and cayenne pepper in your food processor. Run your food processor until all of the ingredients are well blended and a smooth thick sauce or dip develops. Test and add salt if needed. Transfer to your small-sized bowl or container, cover and refrigerate for at least 1 hour or until ready to use.

2. In your small-sized bowl, mix together your minced garlic, spices, and 3 tablespoons olive oil. Pat your chicken thighs dry and rub each with your garlic-spice mixture.

3. Place your spiced chicken thighs in your large-sized tray on a bed of sliced red onions with lemon juice and your remaining 2 tablespoons of olive oil. Cover and refrigerate for at least 4 hours.

4. When ready, heat your gas grill to a medium-high. Place your chicken thighs on your grill. Cover for approximately 5 to 6 minutes, then turn your chicken over and grill for another 5 to 6 minutes covered.

5. Add your dill Greek yogurt dip on the side.

6. Serve!

Oven Puttanesca (Serves 6)

Ingredients:

12 ounces of Gluten-Free Penne

3 tablespoons of Rinsed Capers

6 Tomatoes (Cut Into 1-Inch Wedges)

2 cloves of Thinly Sliced Garlic

1/3 cup of Pitted Kalamata Olives (Halved)

2 tablespoons of Extra-Virgin Olive Oil

Kosher Salt

Ground Pepper

Directions:

1. Preheat your oven to 425 degrees.

2. Toss your tomatoes, capers, garlic, oil, pepper, and salt on your baking sheet. Roast for approximately 35 minutes, then reduce your heat to 375 degrees. Add your olives, stirring at least once, and roast approximately 15 more minutes.

3. Meanwhile, bring your large-sized pot of water to a boil. Add your pasta and cook for about 8 to 10 minutes until al dente. Drain.

4. Toss your pasta with your tomato sauce, and season with your pepper and salt. Drizzle olive oil on top as desired.

5. Serve!

Briam (Serves 6)

Ingredients:

6 Medium Tomatoes (Thinly Sliced)

Large Aubergine (Halved Length-Wise & Thickly Sliced)

2 pounds of Large Potatoes (Chopped Into Cubes)

5 ounces of Extra-Virgin Olive Oil

3 cloves of Garlic (Sliced)

12 Cherry Tomatoes

11 Large Onion (Thinly Sliced)

10.5 ounces of Tomato Passata

5 Courgettes (Sliced)

2 tablespoons of Flat-Leaf Parsley (Finely Chopped)

1 tablespoon of Dried Oregano

Directions:

1. Preheat your oven to 425 degrees. Heat your olive oil in your frying pan over a medium heat and cook your aubergine in batches, adding more oil if necessary until softened and golden. Should take 5 to 7 minutes. Using a slotted spoon, transfer to your large-sized bowl.

2. Add your onion and garlic to your pan, with a little more oil if necessary and saute until softened. Should take approximately 5 minutes.

3. Transfer to your bowl with the aubergine. Add your potato, tomatoes, water, courgette, passata, and to your bowl. Sprinkle with your oregano and parsley and season generously with sea salt and ground black pepper. Combine well with your hands and transfer to your large-sized oven proof dish. Drizzle with any remaining oil.

4. Bake for approximately 30 minutes then turn oven down to 400 degrees. Bake for another 20 to 30 minutes, or until the top has browned and your vegetables are tender. Allow it to cool slightly.

5. Serve!

Lemon Caper Chicken (Serves 4)

Ingredients:

1 1/2 pounds of Skinless Boneless Chicken Breast Halves (Pounded 3/4 Inch Thick & Cut Into Pieces)

1/4 cup of Capers

2 Eggs

2 tablespoons of Olive Oil

1 cup of Dry Bread Crumbs

1/2 teaspoon of Ground Black Pepper

2 Lemons (Cut Into Wedges)

Directions:

1. Beat your eggs and black pepper together in your bowl. Place your bread crumbs in a separate bowl.

2. Heat your olive oil over a medium heat in your large-sized skillet. Dip each piece of your chicken into your egg mixture and press into your bread crumbs. Brush your loose bread crumbs off your chicken and place the pieces into your hot oil. Fry in your pan for approximately 5 to 8 minutes per side until golden brown. Remove your chicken from the heat.

3. Arrange your chicken pieces on your platter, drizzle a small amount of your caper juice over your chicken. Top with your capers and add your lemon wedges.

4. Serve!

Slow Cooker Rosemary & Red Pepper Chicken (Serves 8)

Ingredients:

8 4-ounce Skinless Boneless Chicken Breast Halves

1 Medium Thinly Sliced Red Bell Pepper (Seeded)

1/4 cup of Dry Vermouth

1 Small Thinly Sliced Onion

1/2 teaspoon of Dried Oregano

4 cloves of Minced Garlic

8 ounces of Turkey Italian Sausages (Casings Removed)

2 teaspoons of Dried Rosemary

1/4 cup of Chopped Fresh Parsley

1 1/2 tablespoons of Cornstarch

2 tablespoons of Cold Water

1/4 teaspoon of Coarsely Ground Pepper

Salt

Directions:

1. In your 6-quart slow cooker, combine your onion, bell pepper, rosemary, garlic, and oregano. Crumble your sausages over your onion mixture.

2. Rinse your chicken and pat it dry. Arrange in a single layer over your sausage. Sprinkle with your pepper. Pour in your vermouth. Cover and cook for approximately 5 to 7 hours on the low setting. Chicken should be tender and cooked through when done.

3. Transfer your chicken to your warm platter and cover to keep it warm.

4. In your bowl, stir together your cold water and cornstarch. Stir your cooking liquid in your slow cooker. Increase the heat to high and cover. Cook, stirring a few times until your sauce has thickened. Should take around 10 minutes.

5. Season with salt. Spoon your sauce over your chicken and sprinkle with your parsley.

6. Serve!

Moussaka (Serves 6)

Ingredients:

1 pound of Ground Turkey

2 cups of Plain Nonfat Yogurt

28-ounce can of Whole Peeled Tomatoes (Chopped Coarsely)

2 Medium Eggplants

1 teaspoon of Ground Cinnamon

1/4 cup of Grated Parmesan Cheese

1 Yellow Onion (Cut Into 1/4-Inch Dice)

1 clove of Minced Garlic

1/4 cup of Chopped Fresh Oregano

1/4 teaspoon of Ground Nutmeg

1/2 cup of Chopped Fresh Flat-Leaf Parsley

1/4 cup of Tomato Paste

1 /4 teaspoon of Ground Pepper

1 teaspoon of Coarse Salt

Olive Oil

Directions:

1. Drain your yogurt into a cheesecloth-lined sieve until it is thickened. At least 2 hours or overnight.

2. Place your turkey in your medium-sized saucepan over a medium heat. Cook your turkey until it is browned. Should take approximately 6 minutes. Using your slotted spoon, transfer over to your medium-sized bowl. Add your garlic, onion, salt, pepper, nutmeg, and cinnamon to your saucepan. Cook for approximately 10 minutes until your onion is translucent. Return your turkey to your saucepan with tomato paste, tomatoes, and oregano. Bring it to a boil, reduce your heat to a medium-low. Simmer until your sauce has thickened. Should take approximately 1 hour. Remove it from the heat. Stir in your chopped parsley. Set to the side.

3. Preheat your broiler. While your sauce cooks, cut your eggplants into 1/4-inch slices. Sprinkle both sides with salt. Place in your colander over your bowl. Allow it to stand for about 1 hour to drain. Discard your liquid and rinse each slice under cold water to remove all the juice and salt. Place your slices on a few layers of paper towels. Press out the water. Lay your dried slices on your baking sheet. Coat it with olive oil and broil for approximately 2 minutes until browned. Turn your slices and coat with your olive oil. Broil for another 2 minutes until browned. Repeat until all of your slices are broiled. Set your cooked eggplant to the side.

4. Place your drained yogurt in your small-sized bowl. Add your eggs and Parmesan. Whisk together briskly. Set to the side.

5. Preheat your oven to 400 degrees. Place a layer of eggplant on the bottom of your 8x8-inch baking pan. Cover with half of your turkey sauce. Place another layer of eggplant slices on top, followed by your remaining turkey sauce. Add a final eggplant layer and cover with your yogurt mixture. Bake for approximately 30 minutes until the top starts to brown and your mixture is bubbling. Transfer to a heat-proof surface. Allow it to rest for about 10 minutes until it cools and begins to get firm. Cut into squares.

6. Serve!

Greek Island Chicken Shish Kebabs (Serves 6)

Ingredients:

2 pounds of Skinless Boneless Chicken Breast (Cut Into 1 1/2-Inch Pieces)

2 Large Red Bell Peppers (Cut Into 1-Inch Pieces)

12 Cherry Tomatoes

1 Large Onion (Quartered)

1 teaspoon of Ground Cumin

12 Fresh Mushrooms

1 teaspoon of Dried Oregano

2 cloves of Minced Garlic

1/4 cup of Lemon Juice

1/4 cup of White Vinegar

1/2 teaspoon of Dried Thyme

1/4 cup of Olive Oil

1/4 teaspoon of Salt

1/4 teaspoon of Ground Black Pepper

6 Wooden Skewers

Directions:

1. Whisk your olive oil, vinegar, cumin, lemon juice, thyme, garlic, black pepper, oregano, and salt together in your large-sized glass bowl. Add your chicken and toss to coat evenly. Cover your bowl with plastic wrap. Marinate for about 2 hours in your refrigerator.

2. Soak your wooden skewers in water for approximately 30 minutes before using.

3. Preheat your outdoor grill to a medium-high heat. Lightly oil your grate.

4. Remove your chicken from your marinade and shake any excess liquid off. Discard your remaining marinade. Alternately thread pieces of your marinated chicken with pieces of your bell pepper, onion, tomatoes, and mushrooms onto your skewers.

5. Cook your skewers on your grill, turning often until browned nicely on all sides. The chicken should no longer be pink in the center. Should take approximately 10 minutes.

6. Serve!

Penne with Shrimp (Serves 8)

Ingredients:

1 pound of Peeled & Deveined Shrimp

1 cup of Grated Parmesan Cheese

16-ounce package of Penne Pasta

2 14.5-ounce cans of Diced Tomatoes

1 tablespoon of Chopped Garlic

1/4 cup of Chopped Red Onion

1/4 cup of White Wine

2 tablespoons of Olive Oil

Directions:

1. Bring your large-sized pot of lightly salted water to a boil. Add your pasta and cook for approximately 8 to 10 minutes until al dente. Drain.

2. Heat your oil over a medium heat in your skillet. Stir in your garlic and onion. Cook until your onion is tender. Mix in your tomatoes and wine. Continue to cook for another 10 minutes. Stir occasionally.

3. Mix your shrimp into your skillet and cook for approximately 5 minutes until opaque. Toss with your pasta and top with your Parmesan cheese.

4. Serve!

Spicy Mediterranean Chicken with Sausage-Stuffed Cherry Peppers (Serves 6)

Ingredients:

6 4-ounce Bone-In Chicken Thighs w/ Skin

18 Cherry Peppers (In Brine)

2 tablespoons of Ground Cumin

2 cups of Chicken Stock

6 ounces of Fresh Italian Sausage

14-ounce can of Artichoke Hearts (Drained & Chopped)

1 Sliced Onion

2 tablespoons of Olive Oil

1/2 teaspoon of Crushed Red Pepper Flakes

4 cloves of Crushed Garlic

1 cup of Sliced Pepperoncini Peppers w/ Juices

1/2 cup of Pitted Kalamata Olives

1 tablespoon of Herbes De Provence

1 tablespoon of Chopped Fresh Basil

1 tablespoon of Chopped Fresh Oregano

1 tablespoon of Chopped Fresh Marjoram

1 tablespoon of Ground Black Pepper

1 teaspoon of Salt

Directions:

1. Preheat your oven to 350 degrees.

2. Place your chicken thighs in your large-sized bowl. Season with your cumin, salt, and black pepper. Set to the side.

3. Stuff each of your cherry peppers generously with your Italian sausage. Set to the side.

4. Heat your olive oil in your Dutch oven over a medium-high heat. Place your chicken thighs, facing skin-side down, in your pan and cook for about 5 minutes until brown. Turn the chicken over and brown the other side for about 1 minute. Remove your chicken from the pan.

5. Cook your onion in your Dutch oven over a medium-high heat. Cook and stir for approximately 5 minutes until your onion has caramelized. Reduce your heat to medium and stir in your herbes de Provence, garlic, and crushed red pepper.

6. Stir in the pepperoncini and its juices. Cook for approximately 2 minutes until warmed through. Remove from the heat.

7. Place your chicken, skin-side up, in a single layer over top your onions and pepperoncini in the Dutch oven. Pour your stock into the pan until it is nearly covering the chicken.

8. Sprinkle your olives, artichoke hearts, and stuffed cherry peppers over top of the chicken.

9. Return to a medium-high heat and bring it to a simmer.

10. Cover and roast in your preheated oven for approximately 1 hour until the sausage is cooked through and the liquid is bubbling.

11. Garnish with your oregano, chopped basil, and marjoram.

12. Serve!

Skillet Gnocchi w/ Shrimp & Asparagus (Serves 4)

Ingredients:

1 pound of Peeled & Deveined Raw Shrimp

16-ounce package of Shelf-Stable Gnocchi

1/3 cup of Grated Parmesan Cheese

1 tablespoon + 2 teaspoons of Extra-Virgin Olive Oil

1/2 cup of Sliced Shallots

1 bunch of Trimmed Asparagus (Cut Into Thirds)

3/4 cup of Reduced-Sodium Chicken Broth

2 tablespoons of Lemon Juice

1/4 teaspoon of Ground Pepper

Pinch of Salt

Directions:

1. Heat 1 tablespoon of your oil in your large-sized nonstick skillet over a medium heat. Add your gnocchi and cook, stirring often, until plumped and golden. Should take approximately 6 to 10 minutes. Transfer over to your bowl.

2. Add your remaining 2 teaspoons of oil and your shallots to the pan. Cook over a medium heat, stirring, until beginning to brown. Should take approximately 1 to 2 minutes. Stir in your broth and asparagus. Cover and cook until your asparagus is barely tender. Should take approximately 3 to 4 minutes. Add your shrimp, salt, and pepper. Cover and simmer until your shrimp is pink and cooked through. Should take approximately 3 to 4 minutes more.

3. Return your gnocchi to your skillet along with your lemon juice and cook for 2 minutes, stirring, until heated through. Remove from the heat. Sprinkle with Parmesan cheese, cover and allow to stand for about 2 minutes until the cheese is melted.

4. Serve!

Shrimps Saganaki (Serves 4)

Ingredients:

1 pound of Medium Shrimps w/ Shells

14.5-ounce can of Diced Tomatoes

1 Chopped Onion

8-ounce package of Feta Cheese

1 cup of White Wine

1/4 teaspoon of Garlic Powder

2 tablespoons of Chopped Fresh Parsley

1/4 cup of Olive Oil

Pepper

Cubed Salt

Directions:

1. Bring 2-inches of water to a boil in your large-sized saucepan. Add your shrimp, the water should barely cover them. Boil for approximately 5 minutes. Drain and reserve your liquid. Set to the side.

2. Heat 2 tablespoons of your oil in a saucepan. Add your onions. Cook until your onions are soft. Mix in your wine, parsley, garlic powder, tomatoes, and your remaining olive oil. Simmer for approximately 30 minutes, stirring occasionally until your sauce has thickened.

3. While your sauce is simmering, remove the legs of the shrimp and pull off your shells, leaving the head and tail. You can remove the legs by pinching them.

4. Once the sauce has thickened, stir in your shrimp and shrimp stock. Bring it to a simmer and cook for approximately 5 minutes. Add your feta cheese and remove it from the heat. Allow it to stand until the cheese begins to melt.

5. Serve!

Simple Mediterranean Fish (Serves 4)

Ingredients:

4 6-ounce Halibut Fillets

5-ounce jar of Pitted Kalamata Olives

1 Chopped Onion

1 Large Chopped Tomato

1 tablespoon of Lemon Juice

1 tablespoon of Greek Seasoning

1/4 cup of Capers

1/4 cup of Olive Oil

Salt

Pepper

Directions:

1. Preheat your oven to 350 degrees.

2. Place your halibut fillets on your sheet of aluminum foil and season using your Greek seasoning.

3. Combine your tomato, olives, onion, capers, lemon juice, olive oil, pepper, and salt in a bowl. Spoon your mixture over the halibut. Carefully seal the edges of your aluminum foil to create a packet. Place the packet on your baking sheet.

4. Bake for approximately 30 to 40 minutes until your fish flakes easily with a fork.

5. Serve!

Baked Italian Chili Chicken (Serves 1)

Ingredients:

4 1/2 ounces of Boneless Skinless Chicken Breast

1/2 Red Chili (Thinly Sliced)

8 Olives

5 Shredded Basil Leaves

1 teaspoon of Olive Oil

5 Cherry Tomatoes (Cut In Half)

Pinch of Pepper

1/4 teaspoon of Salt

Directions:

1. Heat your oven to 425 degrees.

2. Trim any fat off your chicken and pop in your small-sized baking dish.

3. On top of your chicken put your tomato, chili, basil, and olives.

4. Drizzle your olive oil over your chicken and season with your salt and pepper.

5. Pop your baking dish in your oven and cook for approximately 25 minutes.

6. Check that your chicken is cooked through. If not then pop it back in your oven for a few minutes.

7. Add your crusty bread or a baked potato to soak up your juices on the side if you so desire.

8. Serve!

Flounder Mediterranean (Serves 4)

Ingredients:

1 pound of Flounder Fillets

24 Pitted & Chopped Kalamata Olives

1/2 of a Spanish Onion

3 tablespoons of Freshly Grated Parmesan Cheese

5 Roma Tomatoes

2 tablespoons of Extra-Virgin Olive Oil

6 leaves of Fresh Basil (Torn)

2 cloves of Chopped Garlic

1/4 cup of Capers

1 teaspoon of Fresh Lemon Juice

1/4 cup of White Wine

6 leaves of Fresh Basil (Chopped)

Pinch of Italian Seasoning

Directions:

1. Preheat your oven to approximately 425 degrees.

2. Bring your saucepan of water to a boil. Put your tomatoes into your boiling water and immediately remove to your bowl of ice water. Drain the water. Remove and discard your skins from the tomatoes. Chop your tomatoes and set to the side.

3. Heat your olive oil over a medium heat in your skillet. Saute your onion for approximately 5 minutes until tender. Stir in your garlic, tomatoes, and Italian seasoning. Cook for approximately 5 to 7 minutes until your tomatoes are tender. Mix in your wine, olives, lemon juice, capers, and chopped basil. Reduce the heat, blend in your Parmesan cheese, and cook until your mixture is reduced to a thick sauce. Should take approximately 15 minutes.

4. Place your flounder in your shallow baking dish. Pour your sauce over the fillets and top with your torn basil leaves.

5. Bake for approximately 12 minutes. Once finished, the fish should be easily flaked using your fork.

6. Serve!

Sweet Sausage Marsala (Serves 6)

Ingredients:

16-ounce package of Farfalle Pasta

1 Sliced Medium Green Bell Pepper

1 pound of Mild Italian Sausage Links

14.5-ounce can of Italian Style Diced Tomatoes

1 clove of Minced Garlic

14.5-ounce can of Italian Style Diced Tomatoes

1/2 of Sliced Large Onion

1 tablespoon of Marsala Wine

1/3 cup of Water

1 Sliced Medium Red Bell Pepper

Pinch of Dried Oregano

Pinch of Black Pepper

Directions:

1. Bring your pot of water to a boil. Cook your pasta until al dente. Should take approximately 8 to 10 minutes. Drain your pasta.

2. Place your sausages and 1/3 cup of water in your skillet over a medium-high heat. Cover and cook for approximately 5 to 8 minutes. Drain and slice thinly.

3. Return your sausage to your skillet. Stir in your onions, garlic, Marsala wine, and peppers. Cook over a medium-high heat. Stir frequently until your sausage is cooked through. Stir in your black pepper, diced tomatoes, and oregano. Cook for another 2 minutes. Remove from the heat. Add over top your cooked pasta.

4. Serve!

Mediterranean Chicken w/ Eggplant (Serves 5)

Ingredients:

6 Diced Skinless Boneless Chicken Breast Halves

3 Peeled Eggplants (Cut Lengthwise Into 1/2 Inch Thick Slices)

2 tablespoons of Tomato Paste

1 Diced Onion

3 tablespoons of Olive Oil

1/2 cup of Water

2 teaspoons of Dried Oregano

Salt

Pepper

Directions:

1. Place your eggplant strips in your large-sized pot of lightly salted water and allow to soak for approximately 30 minutes.

2. Remove your eggplant from your pot and lightly brush with olive oil. Saute your eggplant until lightly browned. Place in a 9x13-inch baking dish. Set to the side.

3. Saute your onion and diced chicken in your large-sized skillet over a medium heat. Stir in your water and tomato paste. Cover your skillet and reduce the heat to low. Allow it to simmer for approximately 10 minutes.

4. Preheat your oven to 400 degrees. Pour your chicken / tomato mixture over your eggplant. Season with salt, pepper, and oregano. Cover with aluminum foil. Bake for approximately 20 minutes.

5. Serve!

Spanish Cod (Serves 6)

Ingredients:

6 4-ounce Cod Fillets

15 Cherry Tomatoes (Halved)

1 tablespoon of Butter

1 cup of Tomato Sauce

2 tablespoons of Chopped Fresh Garlic

1 tablespoon of Olive Oil

1/4 cup of Finely Chopped Onion

1/4 cup of Deli Marinated Italian Vegetable Salad (Coarsely Chopped)

1/2 cup of Chopped Green Olives

Dash of Cayenne Pepper

Dash of Paprika

Dash of Black Pepper

Directions:

1. Heat your olive oil and butter over a medium heat in your large-sized skillet. Cook your garlic and onions until slightly tender. Stir occasionally. Don't burn the garlic. Add your cherry tomatoes and tomato sauce. Bring it to a simmer. Stir in your marinated vegetable salad and green olives. Season with your cayenne pepper, black pepper, and paprika.

2. Cook your fillets for approximately 5 to 8 minutes in the sauce over a medium heat.

3. Serve!

Mussels Marinara di Amore (Serves 4)

Ingredients:

8 ounces of Linguini Pasta

14.5-ounce can of Crushed Tomatoes

1 pound of Mussels (Cleaned & Debearded)

1 tablespoon of Olive Oil

1 clove of Minced Garlic

1/2 teaspoon of Dried Basil

1/4 cup of White Wine

1/2 teaspoon of Dried Oregano

1 Lemon (Cut Into Wedges)

Pinch of Crushed Red Pepper Flakes

Directions:

1. In your large-sized skillet over a medium heat, warm your oil and saute your garlic until it is transparent.

2. Add your oregano, tomato, red pepper flakes, and basil to your skillet. Reduce the heat to low and simmer for approximately 5 minutes.

3. Bring your large-sized pot of water to a boil. Cook your pasta for approximately 8 to 10 minutes until al dente. Drain and set to the side.

4. Add your mussels and wine to your skillet. Cover and increase the heat to high for approximately 3 to 5 minutes until your mussel shells have opened.

5. Pour mussels mixture over your pasta and sprinkle with parsley. Squeeze your lemon wedges over top of it. Garnish with your remaining lemon.

6. Serve!

Curry Salmon with Napa Slaw

Ingredients:

4 6-ounce Salmon Fillets

1 pound of Thinly Sliced Napa Cabbage

1 cup of Brown Basmati Rice

1 pound of Grated Carrots

2 teaspoons of Curry Powder

2 tablespoons of Grape Seed Oil

1/2 cup of Fresh Mint Leaves

1/4 cup of Lime Juice

Ground Pepper

Coarse Salt

Directions:

1. In your saucepan, bring 2 cups of water to a boil. Add your rice and season with pepper and salt. Cover saucepan and reduce heat to a medium-low. Cook for approximately 30 to 35 minutes until tender.

2. In your large-sized bowl, combine your carrots, cabbage, lime juice, mint, and oil. Season with your pepper and salt. Toss to combine.

3. Heat your broiler and set your rack 4-inches from the heat. Approximately 10 minutes before rice is finished cooking, place your salmon on your baking sheet lined with foil. Rub your salmon with curry. Season with pepper, and salt. Broil for approximately 6 to 8 minutes until cooked through.

4. Fluff your rice with a fork and add it alongside your salad and fish.

5. Serve!

Greek Pasta w/ White Beans & Tomatoes (Serves 4)

Ingredients:

8 ounces of Penne Pasta

19-ounce can of Cannellini Beans

2 14.5-ounce cans of Italian-Style Diced Tomatoes

1/2 cup of Crumbled Feta Cheese

10 ounces of Chopped Fresh Spinach

Directions:

1. Cook your pasta in your large-sized pot of boiling salted water until al dente.

2. Combine your beans and tomatoes in your large-sized skillet. Bring to a boil over a medium-high heat. Reduce the heat and allow it to simmer for 10 minutes.

3. Add spinach to your sauce. Cook for approximately 2 minutes until wilted. Stir constantly.

4. Add your sauce over top of the pasta. Sprinkle with feta cheese.

5. Serve!

Mustard Trout and Lady Apples (Serves 4)

Ingredients:

8 3-ounce Trout Fillets

1 cup of Apple Cider

4 Lady Apples (Cut In Half)

3 tablespoons of Fine Plain Bread Crumbs

1 Minced Shallot

1 tablespoon of Melted Unsalted Butter

2 tablespoons of Extra-Virgin Olive Oil

1 tablespoon of Dijon Mustard

1 teaspoon of Chopped Fresh Thyme

1 tablespoon of Rinsed Capers

2 teaspoons of Light Brown Sugar

Coarse Salt

Pepper

Directions:

1. Preheat your oven to 375 degrees. In your small-sized bowl, combine your thyme, bread crumbs, and shallot. Season with pepper and salt. Add your butter and toss well to combine.

2. Place all of your apples cut-side up in your large-sized baking dish. Sprinkle with sugar and top with your bread crumb mixture. Pour 1/4 cup of cider around the apples. Cover and bake for approximately 30 minutes. Uncover and bake for 20 minutes more until the apples are tender and the crumbs are crispy. Remove it from the oven.

3. Turn oven to a broil and place your rack 4-inches from the heat source. Pat your trout fillets dry. Season each side with your pepper and salt. Brush your baking sheet with 1 tablespoon of oil. Place your trout skin-side up on your baking sheet. Brush your trout skin with your remaining 1 tablespoon of oil. Broil for approximately 6 minutes until the trout is cooked through. Reheat your apples on the shelf directly underneath the trout so your crumbs don't burn for the last 1 to 2 minutes.

4. In your small-sized saucepan, whisk 3/4 cup of cider, capers, and mustard until combined. Cook over a medium-high heat for 5 to 7 minutes until reduced to a sauce consistency. Place 2 trout fillets side by side on each of your 4 plates. Spoon the juices around the fish, Set the 2 apple halves next to each of your fillets.

5. Serve!

Grilled Sardines over Wilted Baby Arugula (Serves 4)

Ingredients:

16 Fresh Sardines (Innards & Gills Removed)

2 Large Bunches of Trimmed Baby Arugula

2 teaspoons of Extra-Virgin Olive Oil

Kosher Salt

Ground Pepper

Lemon Wedges (For Garnish)

Directions:

1. Prepare your grill or griddle. Rinse your arugula, shaking off the excess water. Arrange on your platter and set to the side.

2. Rinse your sardines in cold water, rubbing them to remove your scales. Wipe them dry. In your bowl, combine the olive oil and sardines. Toss well to coat.

3. Grill the sardines over a high heat or hot coals for approximately 2 to 3 minutes per side. Sardines are done once they are golden and crispy. Season with your pepper and salt. Transfer them to your arugula-lined platter and add lemon wedges as a garnish.

4. Serve!

Greek Penne and Chicken (Serves 4)

Ingredients:

1 pound of Skinless Boneless Chicken Breast Halves (Cut Into Bite Sized Pieces)

16-ounce package of Penne Pasta

2 cloves of Minced Garlic

1/2 cup of Chopped Red Onion

1 Chopped Tomato

1 1/2 tablespoons of Butter

14-ounce can of Artichoke Hearts

1/2 cup of Crumbled Feta Cheese

3 tablespoons of Chopped Fresh Parsley

1 teaspoon of Dried Oregano

2 tablespoons of Lemon Juice

Salt

Ground Black Pepper

Directions:

1. Cook your pasta in your large-sized pot of boiling salted water until al dente. Drain.

2. In your large-sized skillet over a medium-high heat, melt your butter. Add your garlic and onion. Cook for approximately 2 minutes. Add your chopped chicken and continue to cook until golden brown. Should take approximately 5 to 6 minutes. Stir occasionally.

3. Reduce your heat to a medium-low. Drain and chop your artichoke hearts. Add them to your skillet along with your chopped tomato, fresh parsley, feta cheese, dried oregano, lemon juice, and drained pasta. Cook for 2 to 3 minutes until heated through.

4. Season with your ground black pepper and salt.

5. Serve!

Greek Fava with Grilled Squid (Serves 6)

Ingredients:

12 ounces of Squid (Cleaned)

3/4 cup of Yellow Split Peas

3 tablespoons of Extra-Virgin Olive Oil

2 cups of Vegetable Broth

1 Small Finely Chopped Red Onion

2 tablespoons of Finely Chopped Fresh Parsley

2 tablespoons of Lemon Juice

1 Lemon (Cut Into Wedges)

3/4 teaspoon of Salt

1/4 teaspoon of Ground Pepper

Skewers

Directions:

1. Rinse your split peas under some running water to remove any pebbles or grit.

2. Heat 1 tablespoon of oil over a medium heat in your large-sized saucepan. Add your onion and cook for approximately 5 minutes until softened. Add your split peas and toss to coat. Add your broth and bring to a boil over a high heat. Reduce your heat to a simmer and cover. Cook for approximately 45 minutes to 1 hour, stirring occasionally and skimming any foam off the surface. Split peas should be tender and most of the liquid should be absorbed. If the liquid is gone before the peas are finished add a little more liquid and continue to cook.

3. Cut the body of your squid into 1/2-inch rings, leave the tentacles whole. Combine the tentacles and rings with 1/2 teaspoon of salt, 1 1/2 teaspoons of oil, and 1/4 teaspoon of pepper in a medium-sized bowl. Set to the side.

4. Transfer your peas to a food processor. Add lemon juice, 1 1/2 teaspoons of oil, and the last 1/4 teaspoon of salt. Process your mixture until creamy, with the consistency of mashed potatoes. Spread this mixture onto your serving platter.

5. Preheat your grill to a medium-high heat. Thread your tentacles and squid rings on skewers. Oil your grill rack. Grill your squid, turning once until tender but firm. Should take about 4 minutes in total.

6. Remove your squid from your skewers and arrange on top of your fava mixture. Drizzle your remaining 1 tablespoon of oil on top. Season with pepper and sprinkle with parsley. Add lemon wedges to the side.

7. Serve!

Old-Fashioned Spaghetti & Meatballs (Serves 6)

Ingredients:

Meatballs

4 ounces of Lean Ground Beef

2 Large Egg Whites (Lightly Beaten)

4 ounces of Hot Italian Sausage

1/3 cup of Bulgur

1 Medium Finely Chopped Onion

1/2 cup of Hot Water

1 teaspoon of Dried Oregano

3 cloves of Finely Chopped Garlic

1 cup of Fresh Breadcrumbs

1/2 teaspoon of Salt

1/2 teaspoon of Freshly Ground Pepper

Sauce & Spaghetti

1 pound of Whole Wheat Spaghetti

1/2 cup of Chopped Fresh Parsley

1/2 cup of Freshly Grated Parmesan Cheese

4 cups of Prepared Marinara Sauce

Directions:

1. Combine your water and bulgur in your small-sized bowl. Allow it to stand until your bulgur is tender and all your liquid is absorbed. Should take approximately 30 minutes.

2. Preheat your oven to 350 degrees. Coat your rack with cooking spray and place it over your foil lined baking sheet.

3. Combine your sausage, ground beef, oregano, egg whites, pepper, onion, breadcrumbs, salt, and your soaked bulgur in your large-sized bowl. Mix together well. Form your mixture into 1-inch meatballs. Should make approximately 24 meatballs. Bake for approximately 25 minutes. Blot well with your paper towel.

4. Bring your large-sized pot of water to a boil. Cook your spaghetti for 8 to 10 minutes until tender. Drain and move to your serving bowl.

5. Bring your sauce to a simmer in a Dutch oven. Add your meatballs to the sauce and simmer for approximately 20 minutes while covered. Stir in your parsley.

6. Top your spaghetti with your sauce and meatballs. Add your grated cheese as desired.

7. Serve!

Salmon Panzanella (Serves 4)

<u>Ingredients:</u>

1 pound of Center Cut Salmon (Skinned & Cut Into 4 Portions)

2 Large Tomatoes (Cut Into 1-Inch Pieces)

8 Pitted & Chopped Kalamata Olives

1 tablespoon of Chopped Capers

3 tablespoons of Extra-Virgin Olive Oil

1/4 cup of Thinly Sliced Fresh Basil

3 tablespoons of Red Wine Vinegar

2 slices of Thick Day Old Whole Grain Bread (Cut Into 1-Inch Cubes)

1 Medium Peeled Cucumber (Cut Into 1-Inch Cubes)

1/4 cup of Thinly Sliced Red Onion

1/2 teaspoon of Kosher Salt

Directions:

1. Preheat your grill to high.

2. Whisk your vinegar, capers, olives, and 1/8 teaspoon of pepper in your large-sized bowl. Slowly whisk in your oil until well combined. Add your tomatoes, bread, onion, cucumber, and basil.

3. Oil your grill rack. Season both sides of your salmon with remaining 1/8 teaspoon of pepper and salt. Grill your salmon until it is cooked through. Should take 4 to 5 minutes per side.

4. Divide your salad among 4 separate plates and top each one with a piece of your salmon.

5. Serve!

Seafood Couscous Paella (Serves 2)

Ingredients:

4 ounces of Peeled & Deveined Small Shrimp

1 cup of Canned Diced Tomatoes (No Salt Added w/ Juice)

4 ounces of Bay Scallops (Tough Muscle Removed)

2 teaspoons of Extra-Virgin Olive Oil

1/2 cup of Whole-Wheat Couscous

1 clove of Minced Garlic

1/2 teaspoon of Fennel Seed

1 Medium Chopped Onion

1/2 teaspoon of Dried Thyme

1/4 cup of Vegetable Broth

1/4 teaspoon of Ground Pepper

1/4 teaspoon of Salt

Pinch of Crumbled Saffron Threads

Directions:

1. Heat your oil in a saucepan over a medium heat. Add your onion and cook for approximately 3 minutes, stirring constantly. Add your thyme, garlic, pepper, salt, fennel seed, and saffron. Cook approximately 20 seconds.

2. Stir in your broth and tomatoes. Bring to a simmer. Cover and reduce the heat. Simmer for approximately 2 minutes.

3. Increase your heat to medium, stir in your scallops and cook for around 2 minutes, stirring occasionally. Add your shrimp and cook for 2 more minutes. Stir in your couscous. Cover and remove from the heat. Allow it to stand for 5 minutes. Fluff.

4. Serve!

Mediterranean Whole Wheat Pizza (Serves 4)

Ingredients:

1 Whole Wheat Pizza Crust

1/4 cup of Crumbled Feta Cheese

2 tablespoons of Chopped Kalamata Olives

1/2 cup of Artichoke Hearts (Drained & Pulled Apart)

2 tablespoons of Sliced Pepperoncini

4-ounce jar of Basil Pesto

All Purpose Flour

Directions:

1. Preheat your oven to 450 degrees.

2. Place your pizza crust onto a floured work surface and spread crust with the basil pesto.

3. Arrange your artichoke heart pieces over your pesto. Scatter your pepperoncini slices and kalamata olives over the pizza. Top with your feta cheese.

4. Bake your pizza until the crust is crispy on the bottom and your cheese has melted. Should take approximately 10 to 12 minutes.

5. Serve!

Lemon-Garlic Marinated Shrimp (Serves 12)

Ingredients:

1 1/4 pounds of Cooked Shrimp

3 tablespoons of Minced Garlic

2 tablespoons of Extra-Virgin Olive Oil

1/4 cup of Minced Fresh Parsley

1/4 cup of Lemon Juice

1/2 teaspoon of Pepper

1/2 teaspoon of Kosher Salt

Directions:

1. Place your garlic and oil in your small-sized skillet and cook over a medium heat for 1 minute until fragrant. Add your parsley, lemon juice, pepper, and salt.

2. Toss with your shrimp in your large-sized bowl. Chill until ready to serve.

3. Serve!

Lemon-Garlic Sardine Fettuccine (Serves 4)

Ingredients:

2 4-ounce cans of Boneless Skinless Sardines (Preferably In Tomato Sauce & Flaked)

8 ounces of Whole-Wheat Fettuccine

1 cup of Fresh Whole-Wheat Breadcrumbs

4 cloves of Minced Garlic

1/4 cup of Lemon Juice

4 tablespoons of Extra-Virgin Olive Oil

1/2 cup of Chopped Fresh Parsley

1/4 cup of Finely Shredded Parmesan Cheese

1/2 teaspoon of Salt

1 teaspoon of Ground Pepper

Directions:

1. Bring your large-sized pot of water to a boil. Cook your pasta for approximately 8 to 10 minutes until tender Drain.

2. Heat 2 tablespoons of your oil in your small-sized nonstick skillet over a medium heat. Add your garlic and cook, stirring, until fragrant and sizzling but not yet browned. Should take approximately 20 seconds. Transfer your garlic and oil to your large-sized bowl.

3. Heat your remaining 2 tablespoons of your oil in the pan over a medium heat. Add your breadcrumbs and cook, stirring, until golden brown and crispy. Should take approximately 5 to 6 minutes. Transfer to your plate.

4. Whisk your lemon juice, salt, and pepper into your garlic oil. Add your pasta to the bowl along with your sardines, Parmesan cheese, and parsley. Stir gently to combine. Sprinkle some breadcrumbs on top.

5. Serve!

Linguine w/ Two-Olive Tapenade (Serves 4)

Ingredients:

1/2 pound of Linguine

6-ounce can of Tuna

1 1/2 cups of Cherry Tomatoes (Quartered)

Tapenade

16 Pitted Kalamata Olives

18 Pitted Ripe Green Olives

2 tablespoons + 1/3 cup of Chopped Fresh Flat-Leaf Parsley

1/4 teaspoon of Crushed Red Pepper Flakes

2 cloves of Garlic

Finely Grated Zest of 1 Lemon

1/2 teaspoon of Ground Black Pepper

Directions:

1. Bring your large-sized pot of water to a boil. Add your pasta and cook for approximately 8 to 10 minutes until al dente. Drain your pasta, reserving 1/4 cup of the cooking water.

2. In the bowl of your food processor fitted with a metal blade, combine your lemon zest, olives, garlic, black pepper, red pepper flakes, and 2 tablespoons of parsley. Process until your mixture is combined and finely chopped.

3. Transfer your pasta to your large-sized serving bowl and toss with your reserved cooking water. Add your mixture, tuna, tomatoes, and remaining 1/3 cup of chopped parsley. Toss to coat well.

4. Serve!

Tilapia Feta Florentine (Serves 4)

Ingredients:

1 pound of Tilapia Fillets

1/4 cup of Chopped Onion

2 teaspoons of Olive Oil

1 clove of Minced Garlic

1/4 cup of Kalamata Olives

2 9-ounce bags of Fresh Spinach

2 tablespoons of Crumbled Feta Cheese

1/2 teaspoon of Salt

1/2 teaspoon of Grated Lemon Rind

1/8 teaspoon of White Pepper

2 teaspoons of Lemon Juice

1/4 teaspoon of Dried Oregano

2 tablespoons of Melted Butter

Pinch of Paprika

Directions:

1. Preheat your oven to 400 degrees.

2. Heat your olive oil over your medium heat in your large-sized skillet. Cook and stir your garlic and onion for approximately 5 minutes until your onion is soft. Add your spinach and cook for approximately 5 minutes until the spinach has wilted and cooked down. Stir in your feta cheese, olives, salt, lemon rind, oregano, and white pepper. Continue to cook until your cheese has all melted and the flavors are blended. Should take another 5 minutes.

3. Spread your spinach mixture into a 9x13-inch baking dish. Arrange your fillets over your spinach mixture. Mix together your lemon juice and butter in your small-sized bowl and drizzle over your fish. Sprinkle with a pinch of paprika.

4. Bake your fish for approximately 20 to 25 minutes until the flesh has turned opaque and flakes easily.

5. Serve!

Chapter Four: Mediterranean Diet Sides, Soups, & Snacks Recipes

In this section, I will give you 25+ Mediterranean sides, soups & condiment recipes you can make yourself. I'll include a few basic recipes and a few more advanced recipes. That way no matter what your level in the kitchen you'll be able to prepare yourself something healthy to keep you on track with your diet.

Warm Olives w/ Rosemary

Ingredients:

4 ounces of Green Olives

4 ounces of Black Olives

1/4 teaspoon of Fennel Seeds

1/4 cup of Olive Oil

1 sprig of Rosemary

Pinch of Crushed Red Pepper

Directions:

1. Heat up your ingredients in your skillet over a medium heat. Saute, making sure to toss until it starts to brown. Should take approximately 3 minutes.

2. Allow it to cool to room temperature.

3. Serve!

Steamed Artichokes w/ Aioli (Serves 4)

Ingredients:

3 Large Egg Yolks (Room Temperature)

4 Medium Artichokes

1 tablespoon of Fresh Lemon Juice

1 tablespoon of Finely Chopped Garlic

2 teaspoons of Sherry Vinegar

1 cup of Extra-Virgin Olive Oil

Freshly Ground Black Pepper

Kosher Salt

Directions:

1. Trim about a 1/2-inch off the tops of your artichokes, cut off the stems, and use your kitchen shears to cut off the pointy tips of the outer leaves. Rinse your artichokes.

2. In your large-sized pot, bring about 2-inches of water to a simmer over a medium heat. Set your steamer basket in your pot, add your artichokes, and cover. Steam until an outer leaf pulls out easily. Should take about 30 to 35 minutes.

3. Meanwhile, put your egg yolks, lemon juice, garlic, vinegar, 1/2 teaspoon of salt, and 1/4 teaspoon of pepper in your medium-sized bowl and beat with your hand mixer on medium speed until pale yellow and foamy. Should take about 1 minute.

4. Slowly drizzle in your oil while mixing on medium-high speed until emulsified. If necessary, stir in a some warm water to thin the aioli. One the side, add your steamed artichokes for dipping.

5. Serve!

Bulgur w/ Mushrooms & Cashews (Serves 4)

Ingredients:

2 cups of Vegetable or Chicken Broth

6 ounces of Chopped White Mushrooms

1 cup of Quick-Cooking Bulgur

1 tablespoon of Olive Oil

1/2 cup of Toasted Chopped Unsalted Cashews

1 tablespoon of Unsalted Butter

1/2 cup of Finely Grated Parmigiano-Reggiano

1 teaspoon of Minced Garlic

2 tablespoons of Minced Fresh Parsley

Kosher Salt

Ground Black Pepper

Directions:

1. Bring your vegetable or chicken broth to a boil in your 3-quart saucepan. Stir in your bulgur, reduce the heat to a simmer, cover, and cook until tender and your liquid is absorbed. Should take about 12 minutes.

2. Meanwhile, heat your oil and butter in your 12-inch skillet over a medium heat. Add your mushrooms and cook, undisturbed, until golden on the bottom. Should take about 4 to 5 minutes. Season with your salt and pepper and continue cooking, stirring occasionally, until deep golden brown. Should take about 5 minutes. Add your garlic and cook, stirring, for 1 minute.

3. When your bulgur is cooked, stir in your Parmigiano, then toss with your mushrooms, cashews, and parsley.

4. Serve!

Imam Bayaldi (Serves 8)

Ingredients:

4 Small Italian Eggplants

3/4 cup of Crumbled Feta

10 tablespoons of Extra-Virgin Olive Oil

1 Large Diced Sweet Onion

2 1/2 pounds of Tomatoes (Halved)

1/2 cup of Finely Chopped Cauliflower

1 Medium Diced Green Bell Pepper

1/2 cup of Finely Chopped Fresh Flat-Leaf Parsley

1 tablespoon of Finely Chopped Garlic

1 teaspoon of Finely Chopped Fresh Oregano

Kosher Salt

Directions:

1. Position your rack in the center of your oven and heat the oven to 375 degrees.

2. Halve each of your eggplants lengthwise and place the cut side up on your large rimmed baking sheet. Season the cut sides with salt and brush generously with 4 tablespoons of your oil. Flip your eggplant over and roast, cut side down, until soft. Should take about 35 minutes. Set to the side until cool enough to handle.

3. Grate your cut sides of the tomatoes on the large holes of your box grater. Discard your skins. Drain the pulp in a fine-mesh sieve, stirring occasionally, until most of their liquid has strained through. Should take about 20 minutes.

4. Heat 3 tablespoons of your oil in a 12-inch skillet over a medium heat. Add your onion and cook, stirring occasionally, until soft. Should take about 5 minutes. Add your pepper, cauliflower, and garlic. Cook, stirring occasionally until the vegetables have softened somewhat. Should take another 5 minutes. Remove from the heat. Stir in your tomato pulp, parsley, and oregano, and season with pepper and salt. Stir in your feta.

5. Using your spatula, flip your eggplant over. With a slotted spoon, divide your filling among the eggplant, using the spoon to gently push your filling into the flesh. Drizzle with your remaining 3 tablespoons of oil and bake until hot. Should take about 10 minutes. Sprinkle with crumbled feta and parsley.

6. Serve!

Black Bean Hummus (Serves 8)

Ingredients:

15-ounce can of Black Beans (Drain & Reserve Liquid)

10 Greek Olive

1 clove of Garlic

2 tablespoons of Lemon Juice

3/4 teaspoon of Ground Cumin

1 1/2 tablespoons of Tahini

1/4 teaspoon of Cayenne Pepper

1/4 teaspoon of Paprika

1/2 teaspoon of Salt

Directions:

1. Mince your garlic in your bowl of your food processor. Add your black beans, 2 tablespoons of reserved liquid, lemon juice, tahini, 1/2 teaspoon of ground cumin, salt, and 1/8 teaspoon cayenne pepper. Process ingredients until smooth, scraping down your sides as needed.

2. Add your remaining seasonings and liquid. Garnish with your Greek olives and paprika.

3. Serve!

Sun-Dried Tomato Pesto (Serves 40)

Ingredients:

4 ounces of Sun-Dried Tomatoes

1/2 cup of Grated Parmesan Cheese

2 tablespoons of Chopped Fresh Parsley

1 tablespoon of Tomato Paste

1/4 cup of Chopped Pine Nuts

2 tablespoons of Chopped Fresh Basil

1 tablespoon of Chopped Garlic

1/3 cup of Crushed Tomatoes

1/4 cup of Balsamic Vinegar

3 tablespoons of Chopped Onion

1/4 cup of Red Wine

1/2 cup of Olive Oil

Salt

Directions:

1. Place your sun-dried tomatoes in your bowl and cover them with warm water for approximately 5 minutes, or until tender.

2. In your food processor or blender combine your sun-dried tomatoes, parsley, pine nuts, basil, garlic, and onion. Process ingredients until well blended. Add your vinegar, crushed tomatoes, tomato paste, and red wine. Process ingredients until well blended. Stir in your olive oil and Parmesan cheese. Season with your salt.

3. Serve!

Easy Hummus (Serves 8)

Ingredients:

2 15-ounce cans of Garbanzo Beans (Drained)

1 1/2 teaspoons of Dried Basil

1/4 cup of Chopped Red Onion

1 1/2 teaspoons of Dried Oregano

3 tablespoons of Chopped Roasted Garlic

1 1/2 teaspoons of Dried Parsley

1 tablespoon of Lemon Juice

1 1/2 teaspoons of Dried Sage

1 tablespoon of Olive Oil

Directions:

1. In your food processor or blender, pulse your onions and garlic until finely chopped. Add your garbanzo beans, one can at a time, and pulse to puree. Blend in your basil, lemon juice, sage, oregano, parsley, and oil. Puree ingredients until smooth.

2. Serve!

Smoked Trout & Summer Bean Salad (Serves 10)

Ingredients:

10 ounces of Skinless Smoked Trout Fillet

12 ounces of Green Beans (String Removed If Tough, Cut Into 1/2-Inch Pieces)

1 cup of Plain Greek Yogurt

1/2 cup of Sunflower Seed

1 Large Cucumber (Peeled If Skin Is Tough, Cut Into 1/2-Inch Dice)

4 cups of Cooked Cranberry or Cannellini Beans

1/2 cup of Finely Chopped Red Onion

1 cup of Oil-Cured Black Olives (Pitted & Halved)

1/4 cup + 1 teaspoon of Chopped Fresh Parsley

3 tablespoons of Fresh Lemon Juice

1/2 cup of Toasted Sunflower Seeds

2 tablespoons + 1 teaspoon of Fresh Marjoram Leaves (Coarsely Chopped)

1/4 cup + 1 teaspoon of Chopped Fresh Dill

2 cloves of Garlic (Finely Chopped)

3 tablespoons of Red Wine Vinegar

1 tablespoon of Finely Grated Lemon Zest

Kosher

Sea Salt

Directions:

1. In your 12-inch skillet, cook your green beans in the oil over a medium heat until they begin to sizzle. Should take about 1 minute. Add 1 tablespoon of water, cover, and steam until crisp-tender. Should take about 4 minutes. Transfer to your large-sized bowl and let it cool to room temperature. Should take about 15 minutes.

2. Add your cranberry beans, olives, cucumber, parsley, onion, sunflower seeds, lemon juice, dill, lemon zest, vinegar, marjoram, and garlic. Season with your salt and pepper and mix gently.

3. Arrange your salad on your large-sized serving platter and top with your dollops of yogurt. Crumble your trout into chunks and scatter over the top. Garnish with your reserved herbs and more black pepper.

4. Serve!

Fresh Market Gazpacho (Serves 10)

Ingredients:

5 Large Diced Plum Tomatoes

15.5-ounce can of Garbanzo Beans (Drained & Rinsed)

1 stalk of Diced Celery

2 Chopped Green Onions

1 Cucumber (Peeled, Seeded & Diced)

1/4 cup of Chopped Fresh Parsley

2 tablespoons of Finely Chopped Sweet Onion

1/2 Diced Yellow Bell Pepper

1/2 Diced Red Bell Pepper

46-ounce can of Tomato Juice

1/2 Juiced Lemon

1 clove of Minced Garlic

1 teaspoon of Curry Powder

Dash of Hot Pepper Sauce

Pinch of Dried Tarragon

Ground Black Pepper

Directions:

1. In your large-sized glass bowl, mix your tomatoes, cucumber, celery, garbanzo beans, sweet onion, parsley, yellow bell pepper, red bell pepper, garlic, and lemon juice.

2. Pour in your tomato juice. Season with your curry powder, tarragon, pepper, and hot pepper sauce. Chill in your refrigerator for at least 2 hours.

3. Serve!

Baked Falafel (Serves 2)

Ingredients:

15-ounce can of Garbanzo Beans (Drained & Rinsed)

1 Egg (Beaten)

1/4 cup of Chopped Onion

1/4 teaspoon of Ground Coriander

1/4 cup of Chopped Fresh Parsley

1 teaspoon of Ground Cumin

1 tablespoon of All-Purpose Flour

3 cloves of Minced Garlic

1/4 teaspoon of Baking Soda

2 teaspoons of Olive Oil

1/4 teaspoon of Salt

Directions:

1. Wrap your onion in a cheese cloth and squeeze out as much of the moisture as possible. Set to the side.

2. Place your garbanzo beans, garlic, baking soda, coriander, cumin, parsley, and salt in your food processor. Process until your mixture is coarsely pureed.

3. Mix your garbanzo bean mixture and your onion together in your bowl. Stir in your egg and flour. Shape your mixture into 4 large-sized patties and allow to stand for approximately 15 minutes.

4. Preheat your oven to 400 degrees.

5. Heat your olive oil in an oven-safe skillet over a medium-high heat. Place your patties in your skillet and cook until golden brown. Should take approximately 3 minutes per side.

6. Transfer your skillet to your preheated oven and bake for approximately 10 minutes until heated through.

7. Serve!

Crispy Potatoes w/ Lemon & Oregano (Serves 8)

Ingredients:

1 1/2 pounds of Yukon Gold Potatoes (Well Washed)

2 tablespoons of Fresh Lemon Juice

2 tablespoons of Sherry Vinegar

1 tablespoon of Dijon Mustard

1 tablespoon of Finely Grated Lemon Zest

1/2 cup of Extra-Virgin Olive Oil

1 teaspoon of Honey

1 tablespoon of Dried Oregano

Freshly Ground Black Pepper

Kosher Salt

Directions:

1. In your 8-quart pot, combine your potatoes and enough cold water to cover by 2-inches. Add 1 tablespoon of salt, bring to a boil, reduce to a simmer, and cook until tender enough to be easily pierced with your metal skewer. Should take about 12 to 20 minutes.

2. Meanwhile, in your small-sized bowl, whisk your vinegar, lemon juice and zest, honey, mustard, and a pinch of salt. Slowly whisk in your 1/2 cup of olive oil until your dressing is emulsified. Season with your salt and pepper.

3. Without draining it, transfer your pot to your sink. Slowly cool your potatoes by running cold water into your pot. Should take about 7 minutes. Drain and transfer your potatoes to a cutting board or baking sheet and let them air-dry or pat them dry.

4. Position your rack in the center of your oven and heat your oven to 200 degrees. Place an oven-safe platter on your rack.

5. Using the bottom of your ramekin or bowl, flatten your potatoes to about 1/2-inch thick.

6. Heat 2 tablespoons of oil in your 12-inch heavy-duty skillet over a medium heat. Cook your potatoes in batches of 6 to 8, flipping once about halfway through and adding more oil as needed until golden and crispy on both sides. Should take about 10 minutes total. Transfer to your platter and repeat. Coat your potatoes well with dressing. Crush your oregano between your fingers and sprinkle it over your potatoes.

7. Serve!

Tasty Hummus (Serves 40)

Ingredients:

2 15.5-ounce cans of Garbanzo Beans (Drained)

4 tablespoons of Lemon Juice

6 cloves of Peeled & Crushed Garlic

3 tablespoons of Tahini

1/4 teaspoon of Crushed Red Pepper

Directions:

1. Place your garbanzo beans in your food processor and blend into a spreadable paste. Mix in your lemon juice, tahini, garlic, and crushed red pepper. Blend until smooth, using more lemon juice if your consistency is too thick.

2. Serve!

Greek Tzatziki (Serves 40)

Ingredients:

32-ounce container of Plain Low-Fat Yogurt

1/2 Peeled & Grated English Cucumber

1 clove of Pressed Garlic

2 teaspoons of Grated Lemon Zest

2 tablespoons of Extra-Virgin Olive Oil

3 tablespoons of Chopped Fresh Dill

2 tablespoons of Fresh Lemon Juice

1 tablespoon of Salt

1 tablespoon of Black Pepper

Directions:

1. Stir together your yogurt, cucumber, olive oil, garlic, and lemon juice in your bowl. Add your lemon zest, dill, salt, and pepper. Whisk together until smooth.

2. Pour into your serving dish, cover tightly, and refrigerate at least 8 hours.

3. Serve!

Tuscan White Bean Stew

Ingredients:

1 slice of Whole Grain Bread (Cut Into 1/2-Inch Cubes)

2 cups of Dried Cannellini Beans (Rinsed, Soaked Overnight, & Drained)

6 cloves of Chopped Garlic

2 cloves of Quartered Garlic

1 tablespoon + 6 sprigs of Chopped Fresh Rosemary

3 tablespoons of Extra-Virgin Olive Oil

3 Peeled & Chopped Carrots

1 Bay Leaf

1 1/2 cups of Vegetable Broth

1 Chopped Yellow Onion

6 cups of Water

1 teaspoon of Salt

1/4 teaspoon of Ground Black Pepper

Directions:

1. To make your croutons, heat your olive oil over a medium heat in your large-sized frying pan. Add your 2 cloves of quartered garlic and saute for approximately 1 minute. Remove your pan from the heat and allow it to stand for about 10 minutes, in order to infuse a garlic flavor into your oil. Remove any garlic pieces and discard. Return your pan to a medium heat. Add your bread cubes and saute approximately 3 to 5 minutes, stirring frequently until lightly browned. Transfer to your small-sized bowl and set to the side.

2. In your soup pot over a high heat, combine your white beans, bay leaf, water, and a 1/2 teaspoon of salt. Bring to a boil over a high heat. Reduce your heat to low, cover partially and allow to simmer for 60 to 75 minutes until your beans are tender. Drain your beans, reserving a 1/2 cup of the cooking liquid. Discard your bay leaf. Place your cooked beans into your large-sized bowl and save your cooking pot for later use.

3. In your small-sized bowl, combine your reserved cooking liquid and a 1/2 cup of your cooked beans. Mash together using your fork to form a paste. Stir your bean paste into the cooked beans.

4. Return your cooking pot to your stove top and add your olive oil. Heat over a medium-high heat. Stir in your carrots and onion and saute until your carrots are tender but crisp. Should take approximately 6 to 7 minutes. Stir in your chopped garlic and cook until softened. Should take about 1 minute. Stir in your remaining 1/2 teaspoon of salt, bean mixture, pepper, chopped rosemary, and vegetable broth. Bring to a boil, then reduce your heat to low and simmer until your stew is heated through. Should take approximately 5 minutes.

5. Ladle your stew into your warmed bowls and sprinkle with your croutons. Garnish each of your bowls with one of the rosemary sprigs.

6. Serve!

Fresh Tomato Crostini (Serves 4)

Ingredients:

4 Chopped Plum Tomatoes

1/4 pound of Crusty Italian Peasant Bread (Cut Into 4 Slices & Toasted)

1/4 cup of Minced Fresh Basil

1 clove of Minced Garlic

2 teaspoons of Olive Oil

Ground Pepper

Directions:

1. Combine your tomatoes, oil, garlic, basil, and pepper in your medium-sized bowl. Cover and allow it to stand for 30 minutes. Divide your tomato mixture with any juices among your toast.

2. Serve!

Corn On The Cob w/ Chile, Goat Cheese, & Ham (Serves 4)

Ingredients:

4 slices Serrano Ham (Thinly Sliced)

1/4 cup of Fresh Goat Cheese (Room Temperature)

4 ears of Shucked Corn

2 tablespoons of Minced Fresh Hot Red Chile

1/2 teaspoon of Granulated Sugar

1/2 teaspoon of Red Wine Vinegar

1/4 teaspoon of Minced Garlic

Kosher Salt

Directions:

1. Prepare your medium-high (400 to 475 degree) charcoal or gas grill fire for direct grilling.

2. Combine your goat cheese, vinegar, chile, garlic, sugar, and 1/4 teaspoon of salt in your small-sized bowl until well blended.

3. Grill your corn, turning occasionally, until charred in places and crisp-tender. Should take about 8 minutes.

4. Slather your corn with your goat cheese mixture. Wrap 1 slice of ham around each ear, spiraling it from the bottom to top.

5. Serve!

Mediterranean Red Lentil Bean Soup

Ingredients:

8 cups of Chicken Stock

2 Cubed Ripe Tomatoes

2 Large Diced Onions

1 teaspoon of Ground Cumin

2 tablespoons of Extra-Virgin Olive Oil

1/2 Grated Raw Potato

2 cups of Dried Lentil Beans (Rinsed & Sorted)

2 cups of Fresh Spinach

2 Finely Chopped Carrots

Salt

Pepper

Directions:

1. Soak your lentils for a few hours and throw away your water once done soaking.

2. Boil your lentils until they are half cooked (the cooking time will depend on the size and type of your lentil). Try a lentil to determine the level of doneness.

3. Heat your olive oil in your soup pot. Sauté your diced onions and carrots in your olive oil.

4. Place your stock, tomatoes, spinach, and potato into your pot. Add your cumin, salt, and pepper. Add any additional seasonings if desired.

5. Simmer for approximately 30 to 40 minutes or until your lentils get tender. Add additional water as necessary.

6. Add a dash of olive oil.

7. Serve and Enjoy!

Artichokes Alla Romana (Serves 8)

Ingredients:

4 Large Artichokes

1/3 cup of Grated Parmesan Cheese

2 cups of Fresh Whole-Wheat Breadcrumbs

2 tablespoons of Finely Chopped Flat-Leaf Parsley

1 cup + 3 tablespoons of Vegetable Stock

1 tablespoon of Olive Oil

2 Halved Lemons

1 tablespoon of Grated Lemon Zest

3 cloves of Finely Chopped Garlic

1 teaspoon of Chopped Fresh Oregano

1 cup of Dry White Wine

1 tablespoon of Minced Shallot

1/4 teaspoon of Ground Black Pepper

Directions:

1. Preheat your oven to 400 degrees.

2. In your bowl, combine your olive oil and breadcrumbs. Toss well to coat. Spread your crumbs in your shallow baking pan and put in your oven, stirring once halfway through, until your crumbs are lightly golden. Should take approximately 10 minutes. Set to the side to cool.

3. Working with 1 artichoke at a time, snap off any of their tough outer leaves and trim their stem flush with their base. Cut off the top 1/3 of the leaves using a serrated knife, and trim off any of the remaining thorns with your scissors. Rub the cut edges with your lemon half to prevent discoloration. Separate the inner leaves and pull out any small leaves from the center. Using your melon baller or spoon, scoop out the fuzzy choke, then squeeze some of your lemon juice into the cavity. Trim all your remaining artichokes in the same exact manner.

3. In your large-sized bowl, toss your breadcrumbs with your Parmesan, garlic, pepper, lemon zest, and parsley. Add your 3 tablespoons of vegetable stock, 1 tablespoon at a time, using just enough for your stuffing to begin sticking together in smaller clumps.

4. Using 2/3 of your stuffing, mound it slightly in the center of your artichokes. Then, starting at the bottom, spread the leaves open and spoon a rounded teaspoon of your stuffing near the base of each leaf. (The artichokes can be prepared to this point hours ahead and kept refrigerated.)

5. In your Dutch oven with a tight fit lid, combine your 1 cup of vegetable stock, shallot, oregano, and wine. Bring to a boil, then reduce your heat to low. Arrange your artichokes, stem end down, in the liquid in a single layer. Cover and simmer until all your outer leaves are tender. Should take approximately 45 minutes (add more water if necessary).

6. Transfer your artichokes to your rack and allow it to cool slightly. Cut each of your artichokes into quarters.

7. Serve!

Garbanzo Bean Soup (Serves 4)

Ingredients:

2 15.5-ounce cans of Garbanzo Beans

1 cup of Acini Di Pepe Pasta

14.5-ounce can of Peeled & Diced Tomatoes

2 sprigs of Fresh Rosemary

1 teaspoon of Olive Oil

Salt

Pepper

Directions:

1. Combine your tomatoes, olive oil and 1 1/2 cans of your beans in your large-sized saucepan. Bring to a boil. Puree your remaining 1/2 can of garbanzo beans using a blender or food processor. Stir your puree into your saucepan. Place your sprigs of rosemary into your pan without breaking off any of the leaves.

2. Add your pasta and simmer until your pasta is soft, stirring gently to prevent any sticking. Should take approximately 4 to 10 minutes. Remove your rosemary and season with your salt and pepper.

3. Serve!

Braised Kale w/ Cherry Tomatoes (Serves 4)

Ingredients:

1 pound of Kale (Tough Stems Removed & Leaves Chopped Coarsely)

1 cup of Halved Cherry Tomatoes

4 cloves of Thinly Sliced Garlic

1/2 cup of Vegetable Stock

2 teaspoons of Extra-Virgin Olive Oil

1 tablespoon of Fresh Lemon Juice

1/4 teaspoon of Salt

1/8 teaspoon of Ground Black Pepper

Directions:

1. In your large-sized frying pan, heat your olive oil over a medium heat. Add your garlic and saute for 1 to 2 minutes until lightly golden. Stir in your vegetable stock and kale. Cover, reduce your heat to a medium-low and cook until your kale is wilted and some of its liquid has evaporated. Should take approximately 5 minutes.

2. Stir in your tomatoes and cook uncovered for 5 to 7 minutes until your kale is tender. Remove from your heat and stir in your lemon juice, salt, and pepper.

3. Serve!

Barley & Roasted Tomato Risotto (Serves 8)

Ingredients:

10 Large Plum Tomatoes (Each Peeled & Cut Into 4 Wedges)

1/2 cup of Grated Parmesan Cheese

2 Chopped Shallots

2 cups of Pearl Barley

1 1/2 tablespoons of Chopped Fresh Thyme

1/4 cup of Dry White Wine

2 tablespoons of Extra-Virgin Olive Oil

3 tablespoons of Chopped Fresh Basil + Whole Leaves For Garnish

3 cups of Water

3 tablespoons of Chopped Fresh Flat-Leaf Parsley

4 cups of Vegetable Stock

1/2 teaspoon of Ground Black Pepper

1 teaspoon of Salt

Directions:

1. Preheat your oven to 450 degrees.

2. Arrange your tomatoes on your nonstick baking sheet. Drizzle with a tablespoon of your olive oil and sprinkle with 1/4 teaspoon of your salt and 1/4 teaspoon of your pepper. Gently toss to mix. Roast for approximately 25 to 30 minutes until your tomatoes are softened and starting to brown. Set aside 16 tomato wedges to use as your garnish.

3. In your saucepan, combine your water and vegetable stock and bring to a boil over a high heat. Reduce your heat to low and keep it at a simmer.

4. In your large-sized saucepan, heat your remaining tablespoon of olive oil over a medium heat. Add your chopped shallots and saute for 2 to 3 minutes until translucent and soft. Stir in your white wine and cook until most of your liquid has evaporated. Should take approximately 2 to 3 minutes. Stir in your barley and cook, stirring, for another minute. Stir in your 1/2 cup of stock mixture and cook until your liquid is completely absorbed. Continue to stir in your stock mixture in 1/2 cup increments, cooking until your liquid is absorbed before adding any more. Do this until your barley is tender. Should take approximately 45 to 50 minutes total.

5. Remove from your heat and fold in your tomatoes, parsley, grated cheese, thyme, and chopped basil. Add your remaining 3/4 teaspoon of salt and 1/4 teaspoon of pepper. Stir well to combine.

6. Divide your risotto among warmed up individual shallow bowls. Garnish with your reserved roasted tomato wedges and your whole basil leaves.

7. Serve!

Chickpea and Lentil Bean Soup

Ingredients:

16-ounce can of Chickpeas (Drained & Rinsed)

4 stalks of Diced Celery

2 Diced Large Onions

1 cup of Dried Lentils (Rinsed & Sorted)

3 Cubed Ripe Tomatoes

2 cloves of Minced Garlic

6 cups of Water

2 tablespoons of Extra-Virgin Olive Oil

1/2 teaspoon of Cinnamon

1/2 Sliced Lemon

1/2 cup of Chopped Fresh Parsley

1/2 Juiced Lemon

1 teaspoon of Cumin

1/2 teaspoon of Fresh Ginger

3/4 teaspoon of Turmeric

Salt

Directions:

1. Heat your oil in your soup pot. Add your onions to the oil and sauté for approximately 5 minutes. Add your celery and garlic and sauté until your onions turn golden.

2. Add 6 cups of water, your lentils, and spices. Heat until simmering and then cover your pot. Simmer until your lentils are tender. Should take approximately 30 to 40 minutes. Add your tomatoes and chickpeas. Add any additional water if needed. Add any additional spices if desired.

3. Simmer for approximately 10 to 15 minutes over a low heat. Stir in your lemon juice. Add your parsley and salt.

4. Garnish each serving with 1 or 2 lemon slices.

5. Serve!

Twice-Baked Potatoes w/ Chorizo & Roasted Red Pepper (Serves 8)

Ingredients:

4 Large Russet Potatoes (Scrubbed & Pierced 5 Times With Your Fork)

1 teaspoon of Sweet Smoked Paprika

2 ounces of Softened Unsalted Butter

4 ounces of Coarsely Grated Manchego

1/2 cup of Drained & Diced Roasted Red Pepper

1/2 cup of Cooked & Crumbled Fresh Chorizo

1 teaspoon of Chopped Fresh Flat-Leaf Parsley

1/4 cup of Sour Cream

1 tablespoon of Canola Oil

Kosher Salt

Freshly Ground Black Pepper

Directions:

1. Position your rack in the center of your oven and heat your oven to 400 degrees. Place your potatoes directly on your oven rack and bake until tender when pierced with a fork. Should take about 1 hour 10 minutes. Transfer your potatoes to a cutting board and let it sit until cool enough to handle. Should take about 10 minutes.

2. Cut a 1/2-inch-thick slice lengthwise off the top of each potato. Scrape the flesh from the slices into your large-sized bowl and discard your skins. Spoon the flesh from your potatoes into your bowl, leaving a 1/4-inch shell. Add your butter, paprika, 3/4 teaspoon of salt, and 1/2 teaspoon of pepper and mix with your potato masher until blended. Do not overwork (lumps are fine). Gently fold in half of your cheese, chorizo, red pepper, paprika, sour cream, and parsley with a silicone spatula. Season with your salt and pepper.

3. Using your fingers, rub the outsides of your potato shells with your oil. Distribute the filling among your shells, mounding it, and place on your rimmed baking sheet.

4. Bake your potatoes, uncovered, until heated through. Should take about 25 to 30 minutes. Sprinkle your potatoes with your remaining cheese and bake until your cheese melts and browns lightly in some places. Should take about 2 to 3 minutes more. Garnish your potatoes with parsley. Allow it to sit for 5 to 10 minutes.

5. Serve!

Escarole & Roasted Vegetable Salad w/ Anchovy-Garlic Vinaigrette (Serves 6)

Ingredients:

<u>Anchovy Garlic Vinaigrette:</u>

8 Anchovy Fillets (Patted Dry & Minced)

1 tablespoon of Minced Garlic

2/3 cup of Extra-Virgin Olive Oil

1/3 cup of Red Wine Vinegar

Ground Pepper

<u>Breadcrumb Topping:</u>

1 1/2 cups of Coarse Fresh Breadcrumbs

2 tablespoons of Extra-Virgin Olive Oil

3/4 teaspoon of Ground Pepper

<u>Salad:</u>

4 cups of Cauliflower Florets

8 cups of Coarsely Chopped Escarole

12 Baby Yellow Potatoes

1 cup of Sliced Celery

3 tablespoons of Extra-Virgin Olive Oil

6 cups of Sliced Belgian Endive

8-ounce can of Artichoke Hearts

1/2 teaspoon of Kosher Salt

Directions:

1. To prepare your vinaigrette: Combine your anchovies and garlic in your small-sized saucepan with 1/3 cup of oil. Warm your oil over a medium-low heat for 2 to 4 minutes until fragrant. Remove from heat and whisk in your remaining 1/3 cup of your oil and vinegar. Season with your pepper.

2. To prepare your breadcrumbs: Preheat your oven 350 degrees. Combine your breadcrumbs with pepper and oil in your large-sized bowl. Spread on your rimmed baking sheet. Bake for approximately 15 to 20 minutes, stirring occasionally until golden brown. Transfer your breadcrumbs to your small-sized bowl.

3. To prepare your salad: Increase your oven temperature to 400 degrees. Toss your potatoes and cauliflower with 2 tablespoons of oil and salt in your large-sized bowl. Spread on your baking sheet. Roast for approximately 10 minutes.

4. Cut your artichoke hearts into 3/8-inch-thick slices and toss them with your remaining tablespoon of oil in your large-sized bowl. Add to your baking sheet with your cauliflower and potatoes. Continue roasting for approximately 10 to 15 minutes until tender. Once cool enough to handle, cut your potatoes in half or in quarters.

5. Transfer your cauliflower, potatoes, and artichoke hearts to your large-sized bowl. Add your celery and half of your vinaigrette. Allow it to marinate for approximately 15 minutes, stirring occasionally.

6. Toss your escarole and endive in another large-sized bowl with your remaining vinaigrette. Divide your greens among 6 separate salad plates. Top each portion with about 1 cup of your marinated vegetables and a sprinkling of your toasted breadcrumbs.

7. Serve!

Lebanese Fattoush

Ingredients:

Large Pita Bread (Torn Into Bite-Sized Pieces)

1/2 cup of Crumbled Goat Cheese

1 tablespoon of Lemon Juice

2 tablespoons of Olive Oil

1 tablespoon of Minced Garlic

2 Small Diced Tomatoes

1 cup of Chick Peas (Drained)

1 cup of Shredded Romaine Lettuce

1/2 Diced Cucumber

2 tablespoons of Chopped Fresh Parsley

2 tablespoons of Chopped Fresh Mint

Directions:

1. Toast your pita bread in your warm oven until it turns crisp.

2. Place your cucumber, lettuce, mint, parsley, and tomatoes in your large-sized bowl.

3. Toss with your lemon juice, garlic, and olive oil until well coated.

4. Top with your goat cheese, chick peas, and your toasted pita bread.

5. Serve!

Fish Soup w/ Rotelle

Ingredients:

1 dozen Mussels (Still In Shells)

1 pound of Monkfish

1 Diced Onion

1 cup of Rotelle Pasta

1/2 can of Crushed Tomatoes

2 tablespoons of Extra-Virgin Olive Oil

1/4 teaspoon of Rosemary

1 tablespoon of Minced Garlic

Directions:

1. Sauté your onion and garlic in your olive oil until soft.

2. Add 1 quart of water, tomatoes, pasta, and rosemary. Add your salt and pepper. Cook for approximately 15 minutes.

3. Clean your mussels and cut your fish into bite-sized pieces. Add to your soup and simmer for approximately 10 minutes. All of your mussel shells should be opened at this point. Discard any of the unopened ones.

4. Serve and Enjoy!

Baked Tomato

Ingredients:

2 Large Tomatoes

2 cloves of Finely Chopped Garlic

1 tablespoon of Finely Chopped Basil

Extra Virgin Olive Oil

Salt

Pepper

Directions:

1. Preheat your oven to 400 degrees. Brush the bottom of your baking dish with your olive oil.

2. Slice your tomatoes into 1/2-inch thick slices. Place your tomatoes slices into your baking dish. Sprinkle your garlic and basil onto the tops of your tomatoes. Add your salt and pepper. Drizzle some olive oil over your sliced tomatoes.

3. Bake in your oven for approximately 20 to 25 minutes.

4. Pour your olive oil and tomato juice from the bottom of your pan into your small-sized bowl as a dipping sauce for your warm whole grain bread.

5. Serve!

Chapter Five: Mediterranean Diet Dessert Recipes

In this section, I will give you 20+ Mediterranean dessert recipes you can make yourself. I'll include a few basic recipes and a few more advanced recipes. That way no matter what your level in the kitchen you'll be able to prepare yourself a heart-healthy Mediterranean dessert to keep you on track with your diet.

Ricotta Cake

Ingredients:

3 pounds of Fresh Ricotta Cheese

8 Eggs

1/2 pound of Sugar

Zest of 1 Orange

Zest of 1 Lemon

Butter

Directions:

1. In your bowl mix together all of your ingredients.

2. Coat your bottom and sides of your 9-inch springform pan with butter.

3. Pour your mix into your springform pan.

4. Bake for approximately 30 minutes at 425 degrees. Continue baking for an additional 40 minutes at 380 degrees.

5. Allow it to cool.

6. Serve!

Baked Figs w/ Almonds

Ingredients:

24 Almonds

24 Dried Figs

1 Lemon (Peeled & Cut Into Small Pieces)

Directions:

1. Wash your figs in warm water and dry.

2. Butterfly all your figs and place them on your board.

3. Add several pieces of your lemon peel on one of your butterflied figs.

4. Add an almond on each side of your butterflied fig and cover with the other fig. Press them well together and bake at 200 degrees for 1 hour. They are done once they are golden brown.

5. Serve!

Chocolate Mousse w/ Apples (Serves 8)

<u>Ingredients:</u>

4 Large Apples (Firm)

1/4 cup of Sugar

2 Cinnamon Sticks

<u>Mousse:</u>

5 Egg Whites

3/5 cup of 35% Fat Double Cream

1/2 cup of Butter

25 grams of Apple Flavored Tea

3/4 cup of 55% Cocoa Cooking Chocolate (Broken Into Small Pieces)

1/4 cup of Crystalline Sugar

Directions:

1. Peel your apples and cut each of them into 8 pieces. Put your apple flavored tea into your double cream for 24 hours.

2. Put into your saucepan with your cinnamon and sugar and cover with water. Boil until your apples have softened.

3. Allow it to cool. Fill 8 big wine glasses halfway and refrigerate.

4. Heat your cream and butter together. As soon as it begins to boil, pour it over your cooking chocolate, straining your tea.

5. Stir your mixture well until it becomes smooth and blended.

6. Beat your sugar and egg whites, using your mixer on a low speed until it thickens.

7. Add your meringue mix to your chocolate, mix together well and fill your glasses on top of your apple compote. Allow to cool and garnish with dried slices of apple.

8. Serve!

Apricot & Pistachio Baklava w/ Orange-Cardamom Syrup (Serves 30)

Ingredients:

1 pound of Twin Pack of Phyllo Dough (2 8-Ounce Packs Each With 20 9 x 14 Sheets)

2 1/2 cups of Unsalted & Shelled Raw Pistachios

10 ounces of Unsalted Butter

2 cups of Packed Dried Apricots

2/3 cup of Orange Juice

2 cups of Granulated Sugar

1 1/2 teaspoons of Ground Cardamom

Directions:

1. Thaw your phyllo overnight in your refrigerator. Then put your phyllo box on the counter and allow to come to room temperature. Should take approximately 1 to 2 hours.

2. Put your apricots, pistachios, and sugar in your food processor. Process until your nuts and apricots are both finely chopped (the largest should be the size of a small dried lentil). Should take approximately 30 to 45 seconds. Set to the side.

3. Unfold one pack of your phyllo sheets and stack them so that they lie flat on your work surface. Cover the top with your plastic wrap, letting some excess plastic fall over all four edges. Dampen and wring out your kitchen towel and drape it on top of your plastic wrap. This will hold the plastic in place and prevent your phyllo from drying out.

4. Melt your butter in a small-sized saucepan. Brush the bottom of your 9 x 13-inch metal pan (preferably with straight sides and a light color interior to prevent over browning on your edges) with some of your butter. Remove a sheet of your phyllo from the stack. Re-cover the rest (be sure to cover your remaining sheets each time you remove a new one), and put your sheet in the bottom of your pan. Brush your sheet with some of your melted butter but don't soak your phyllo (remember, you'll have about 40 layers of buttered phyllo by the time you're done). Repeat until you have layered and buttered about half the sheets from your first pack—about 10 sheets in all. If your pan has slightly angled sides, arrange your sheets so the excess falls on the same side of your pan and cut the extra off every few layers with your paring knife. Sprinkle about one-third of the filling evenly over your phyllo.

5. Repeat layering and buttering your remaining sheets from the first pack and sprinkle on another third of your filling. Open, unfold, and cover your second pack of phyllo. Layer and butter it as described above, sprinkling your remaining filling after layering about half the phyllo, and ending with a final layer of phyllo (you may not need all of the butter). Cover loosely and put your pan of baklava in your freezer for approximately 30 minutes (this makes it much easier to cut your pastry).

6. Position your oven rack in the center of your oven and heat your oven to 350 degrees.

7. Before baking, use your thin, sharp knife (I prefer serrated) and a gentle sawing motion to cut your baklava on the diagonal at 1-1/2-inch intervals in a diamond pattern. Try not to compress your pastry by pressing down on it with one hand while cutting with the other. Not only are you cutting serving portions, you are also cutting pathways for your flavored syrup to permeate your pastry, so be sure to cut your pastry all the way to the bottom of your pan. If you have an electric carving knife, this is a great time to use it. Bake your baklava until golden. Should take approximately 40 to 45 minutes. Transfer to your rack and allow to cool completely. Run your knife along the cut lines to help your syrup absorb evenly.

8. Put your sugar and orange juice in your small-sized saucepan and bring to a simmer over a medium heat, stirring occasionally, until your sugar is dissolved and your liquid is clear. Should take about 5 minutes. Remove your pan from your heat and stir in your cardamom. Pour your syrup evenly over the entire surface of your baklava, allowing it to run down into the cut marks and along the sides of your pan. Allow the baklava to cool to room temperature.

9. Serve!

Toasted Bread w/ Chocolate (Serves 8)

Ingredients:

4 ounces of Chopped Bittersweet Chocolate

8 slices of Bread (1/2-Inch Thick)

Kosher Salt

Extra-Virgin Olive Oil

Directions:

1. Position your rack 4-inches from your broiler element and heat to high.

2. Put your bread on your baking sheet and toast until lightly golden on both sides. Should take approximately 1 to 2 minutes per side.

3. Drizzle your bread with olive oil. Distribute your chocolate evenly on top of your bread. Turn off your broiler and return your bread to the oven until the residual heat melts your chocolate. Should take approximately 1 minute.

4. Smooth your chocolate with a knife. Sprinkle a pinch of salt on each slice.

5. Serve!

Classic Baklava (Serves 30)

Ingredients:

1 pound Twin Pack of Phyllo Dough (2 8-Ounce Packs Each With 20 9 x 14 Sheets)

2 cups of Granulated Sugar

1 pound of Unsalted & Shelled Raw Pistachios

10 ounces of Unsalted Butter

1 teaspoon of Ground Cinnamon

1 1/2 teaspoon of Orange Flower Water

1 teaspoon of Ground Cardamom

Directions:

1. Thaw your phyllo overnight in your refrigerator. Then put your phyllo box on the counter and allow to come to room temperature. Should take approximately 1 to 2 hours.

2. Put your pistachios, cinnamon, sugar, and cardamom in your food processor. Process until your nuts are finely chopped (the largest should be the size of a small dried lentil). Should take approximately 15 to 20 seconds. Set to the side.

3. Unfold one pack of your phyllo sheets and stack them so that they lie flat on your work surface. Cover the top with your plastic wrap, letting some excess plastic fall over all four edges. Dampen and wring out your kitchen towel and drape it on top of your plastic wrap. This will hold the plastic in place and prevent your phyllo from drying out.

4. Melt your butter in a small-sized saucepan. Brush the bottom of your 9 x 13-inch metal pan (preferably with straight sides and a light color interior to prevent over browning on your edges) with some of your butter. Remove a sheet of your phyllo from the stack. Re-cover the rest (be sure to cover your remaining sheets each time you remove a new one), and put your sheet in the bottom of your pan. Brush your sheet with some of your melted butter but don't soak your phyllo (remember, you'll have about 40 layers of buttered phyllo by the time you're done). Repeat until you have layered and buttered about half the sheets from your first pack—about 10 sheets in all. If your pan has slightly angled sides, arrange your sheets so the excess falls on the same side of your pan and cut the extra off every few layers with your paring knife. Sprinkle about one-third of the filling evenly over your phyllo.

5. Repeat layering and buttering your remaining sheets from the first pack and sprinkle on another third of your filling. Open, unfold, and cover your second pack of phyllo. Layer and butter it as described above, sprinkling your remaining filling after layering about half the phyllo, and ending with a final layer of phyllo (you may not need all of the butter). Cover loosely and put your pan of baklava in your freezer for approximately 30 minutes (this makes it much easier to cut your pastry).

6. Position your oven rack in the center of your oven and heat your oven to 350 degrees.

7. Before baking, use your thin, sharp knife (I prefer serrated) and a gentle sawing motion to cut your baklava on the diagonal at 1-1/2-inch intervals in a diamond pattern. Try not to compress your pastry by pressing down on it with one hand while cutting with the other. Not only are you cutting serving portions, you are also cutting pathways for your flavored syrup to permeate your pastry, so be sure to cut your pastry all the way to the bottom of your pan. If you have an electric carving knife, this is a great time to use it.

8. Bake your baklava until golden. Should take approximately 40 to 45 minutes. Transfer to your rack and allow to cool completely. Run your knife along the cut lines to help your syrup absorb evenly.

9. Put your sugar and a 2/3 cup of water in a small-sized saucepan and bring to a simmer over a medium heat, stirring occasionally, until your sugar is dissolved and your liquid is clear. Should take about 5 minutes. Remove your pan from the heat and stir in your orange flower water (if using).

10. Pour you syrup evenly over the entire surface of your baklava, allowing it to run down into the cut marks and along the sides of your pan. Allow your baklava to cool to room temperature.

11. Serve!

Simple Bocconotti

Ingredients:

Dough:

2 pounds of Flour

1 3/4 cups of Dry White Wine

1/2 cup of Olive Oil

Filling:

1/2 cup of Sugar

2 1/2 cups of Vin Cotto

1 cup of Almonds

Olive Oil

Zest of 1 Lemon

Directions:

1. In your stand mixer, add your olive oil and wine. Mix together. Add your flour and continue to mix until your flour and your liquids are completely amalgamated and your dough is firm.

2. To prepare your filling, boil your almonds and remove your peel. Once they are cold, put them in your food processor or your blender and chop finely.

3. Put your chopped almonds in your bowl, add your lemon zest, sugar and 1/2 cup of Vin Cotto. Mix until your almonds are fully coated with your Vin Cotto.

4. Cut a small-sized piece of dough and roll it very flat with your rolling pin to about 1/8-inch thick.

5. With a teaspoon, deposit a lump of filling on your dough. Cover your filling with the dough to form a half-moon. Cut your excess dough around the filling with your ravioli cutter. Press around your edges to ensure that your dough is completely attached.

6. Make all your Bocconotti. At the end, using your fork, puncture each Bocconotti 2 times.

7. Prepare your hot oil and fry all your Bocconotti until they turn golden.

8. Allow them to completely cool off.

9. In your pot add 2 cups of your Vin Cotto and bring it to a boil.

10. One or two at a time, add your fried Bocconotti into your hot Vin Cotto and allow them to get completely covered.

11. Remove from your pot and deposit on your platter to cool off.

12. Serve!

Hazelnut & Chocolate Baklava w/ Espresso-Frangelico Syrup (Serves 30)

Ingredients:

1 pound twin pack of Phyllo Dough (2 8-Ounce Packs Each With 20 9 x 14 Sheets)

1 pound of Raw Shelled Hazelnuts

6 ounces of Chopped Semi-Sweet Chocolate

2 teaspoons of Ground Cinnamon

1 3/4 cups of Granulated Sugar

2 tablespoons of Frangelico

10 ounces of Unsalted Butter

2 teaspoons of Instant Espresso Powder

Directions:

1. Thaw your phyllo overnight in your refrigerator. Then put your phyllo box on the counter and allow to come to room temperature. Should take approximately 1 to 2 hours.

2. Put your hazelnuts, sugar, chocolate, and cinnamon in your food processor. Process until your nuts and chocolate are finely chopped (the largest should be the size of a small dried lentil). Should take approximately 15 to 30 seconds. Set to the side.

3. Unfold one pack of your phyllo sheets and stack them so that they lie flat on your work surface. Cover the top with your plastic wrap, letting some excess plastic fall over all four edges. Dampen and wring out your kitchen towel and drape it on top of your plastic wrap. This will hold the plastic in place and prevent your phyllo from drying out.

4. Melt your butter in a small-sized saucepan. Brush the bottom of your 9 x 13-inch metal pan (preferably with straight sides and a light color interior to prevent over browning on your edges) with some of your butter. Remove a sheet of your phyllo from the stack. Re-cover the rest (be sure to cover your remaining sheets each time you remove a new one), and put your sheet in the bottom of your pan. Brush your sheet with some of your melted butter but don't soak your phyllo (remember, you'll have about 40 layers of buttered phyllo by the time you're done). Repeat until you have layered and buttered about half the sheets from your first pack—about 10 sheets in all. If your pan has slightly angled sides, arrange your sheets so the excess falls on the same side of your pan and cut the extra off every few layers with your paring knife. Sprinkle about one-third of the filling evenly over your phyllo.

5. Repeat layering and buttering your remaining sheets from the first pack and sprinkle on another third of your filling. Open, unfold, and cover your second pack of phyllo. Layer and butter it as described above, sprinkling your remaining filling after layering about half the phyllo, and ending with a final layer of phyllo (you may not need all of the butter). Cover loosely and put your pan of baklava in your freezer for approximately 30 minutes (this makes it much easier to cut your pastry).

6. Position your oven rack in the center of your oven and heat your oven to 350 degrees.

7. Before baking, use your thin, sharp knife (I prefer serrated) and a gentle sawing motion to cut your baklava on the diagonal at 1-1/2-inch intervals in a diamond pattern. Try not to compress your pastry by pressing down on it with one hand while cutting with the other. Not only are you cutting serving portions, you are also cutting pathways for your flavored syrup to permeate your pastry, so be sure to cut your pastry all the way to the bottom of your pan. If you have an electric carving knife, this is a great time to use it.

8. Bake your baklava until golden. Should take approximately 40 to 45 minutes. Transfer to your rack and allow to cool completely. Run your knife along the cut lines to help your syrup absorb evenly.

9. Put your sugar, espresso powder and 2/3 cup of water in a small-sized saucepan and bring to a simmer over a medium heat, stirring occasionally, until your sugar is dissolved. Should take about 5 minutes. Remove your pan from the heat and stir in your Frangelico. Pour the syrup evenly over the entire surface of your baklava, allowing it to run down into the cut marks and along the sides of your pan. Allow your baklava to cool to room temperature.

10. Serve!

Sesame-Orange Almond Tuiles (Serves 20)

Ingredients:

10 tablespoons of Granulated Sugar

3/4 cup of Blanched Sliced Almonds

1 1/2 teaspoons of Black Sesame Seeds

3 tablespoons of Unsalted Butter

1/4 cup of All-Purpose Flour

2 tablespoons of White Sesame Seeds

1 tablespoon of Toasted Sesame Oil

3 tablespoons of Freshly Squeezed Orange Juice

Grated Zest of 1 Orange

Directions:

1. In your small-sized saucepan, warm your butter, orange juice, sesame oil, orange zest, and sugar over a low heat until melted and smooth. Remove from your heat and stir in your flour, almonds, and black and white sesame seeds. Let your batter rest for approximately 1 hour at room temperature.

2. Preheat your oven to 375 degrees. Line 2 baking sheets with your parchment paper. Set a rolling pin for shaping your tuiles on your folded dish towel to steady it and have your wire rack ready.

3. Drop level tablespoons of your batter on your prepared baking sheets, placing only 4 on each baking sheet, spacing them evenly apart. Slightly flatten your batter with your dampened fingers.

4. Bake one sheet at a time, rotating your baking sheet midway during the baking process until your cookies are evenly browned. Should take approximately 8 to 9 minutes.

5. Allow to cool briefly, approximately 1 minute. Using your metal spatula, lift each of your cookies off your baking sheet and drape it over the rolling pin. (If the cookies cool and harden before you have time to shape them, they can be softened by putting them back in the oven for another 30 to 45 seconds.) Allow them to cool on the rolling pin, then transfer your tuiles to your wire rack. Repeat this process with the remaining batter.

6. Serve!

Cartellate di Primavera

Ingredients:

2 pounds of Flour

1 3/4 cups of Dry White Wine

1/2 cup of Vin Cotto

1/2 cup of Olive Oil

Olive Oil

Extra-Virgin Olive Oil Gelato or Vanilla Gelato

Directions:

1. In your stand mixer bowl, add your olive oil and wine. Mix them together. Add your flour and continue to mix until your flour and your liquids are completely amalgamated and your dough is firm.

2. Cut a handful of your dough and pass it through your pasta roller set at a 3 until you have a flat and long strip of dough about 3 inches wide and 10 inches long. Lay your strip on your wood board and with your ravioli cutter cut it in squares of 2x2-inches.

3. With the teeth of your fork, puncture each square several times so that when you fry them they will not swell.

4. Fry all your cartellate until lightly golden.

5. Place them on your plate lined with paper towels to absorb any excess oil. Set to the side and allow it to cool.

6. Place one cartellate on your serving plate and add a scoop of your gelato on top. Cover your gelato with another cartellate and garnish with a drizzle of your Vin Cotto and a few drops of your olive oil.

7. Serve!

Honey & Tahini Ganache w/ Toasted Sesame Seeds (Serves 40)

Ingredients:

12 1/2 ounces of Chopped Caribbean 66% Dark Chocolate

3/4 cup of Sesame Seeds

2 1/2 tablespoons of Heather Honey

1/3 cup of Tahini

Directions:

1. In your saucepan, bring 3/4 cup of water and your honey to a simmer. Add your tahini and simmer for approximately 2 minutes. Pour your hot liquid onto your chocolate in a bowl and whisk together until smooth. Allow it to cool before refrigerating for approximately 2 hours to fully set your ganache.

2. Lightly toast your sesame seeds in your dry frying pan until golden but not popping open. Allow it to cool.

3. Take your ganache out of your fridge and scoop out any uneven quenelles and immediately roll them through your toasted sesame seeds.

4. Serve!

Pasta Reale

Ingredients:

3 Egg Whites

1 pound of Almonds

1/2 pound of Sugar

1/2 cup of Sugar (For Glazing)

Zest of 2 Lemons

Silver Mini Dragees

Directions:

1. To prepare your paste, boil your almonds and remove your peel. Once they are cold and somewhat dry, put them in your food processor or your blender and chop finely.

2. Put your chopped almonds in your bowl, add your lemon zest, sugar, and egg whites. Mix until your egg whites dilute your sugar and the mixture becomes a paste.

3. Take a lump of your mixture in your hand, roll it into a ball the size slightly smaller than a golf ball.

4. Roll the ball completely into your 1/2 cup of sugar and place it on your baking sheet.

5. Slightly insert a silver ball on top of each of your balls/cookies.

6. Bake for approximately 30 minutes at 375 degrees. Remove from your oven.

7. Serve!

Purceddi in Vin Cotto

Ingredients:

2 pounds of Flour

2 cups of Vin Cotto

1 3/4 cups of Dry White Wine

1/2 cup of Olive Oil

Olive Oil

Cinnamon Powder

Directions:

1. In your stand mixer bowl, add your olive oil and your wine. Mix together well. Add your flour and continue to mix until your flour and your liquids are completely amalgamated and your dough is firm.

2. Take a small-sized piece of your dough and roll it with your hands on your wood board to create a long stick about 1/2-inch thick.

3. Cut your stick into pieces of about 1/2-inch long each.

4. Take each of your pieces and with your index finger press it against the reverse side of your cheese grater so that you will have lumps on one side and it will be somewhat hollow on the other side.

5. Make all your Purceddi.

6. Fry all your Purceddi in olive oil until they are lightly golden.

7. Heat your Vin Cotto in your pan and while the Vin Cotto is still warm, dip a handful of your Purceddi in the Vin Cotto until they are completely covered. Remove and place on your platter. Add a sprinkle of cinnamon.

8. Serve!

Honey-Vanilla Greek Yogurt Mousse w/ Sticky Balsamic Berries (Serves 4)

Ingredients:

Mousse:

1/2 of a Vanilla Bean

2 cups of Plain Yogurt

1/4 cup of Honey

2 tablespoons of Water

3/4 cup of Cold Heavy Cream

Kosher Salt

Berries:

1 tablespoon of Honey

4 Crushed Amaretti Cookies

2 cups of Mixed Fresh Berries (Raspberries, Strawberries, Blueberries, Blackberries)

1/4 cup of Aged Balsamic Vinegar

Ground Black Pepper

Directions:

1. Set your strainer over your bowl and line with 2 layers of damp cheesecloth or paper towels, allowing for a few inches of overhang. Spoon in your yogurt, cover with your cheesecloth overhang or another paper towel and refrigerate until thick, creamy, and reduced by half. Should take approximately 3 to 4 hours.

2. In your small-sized skillet, combine your honey, 2 tablespoons of water, and 1/8 teaspoon of salt. With the tip of your paring knife, split your vanilla bean lengthwise and scrape the seeds into your skillet. Add the bean, too. Bring to a boil over a medium heat, stirring constantly until the honey has melted. Boil vigorously for approximately one minute, swirling your skillet, then remove from the heat. Allow it to cool to room temperature for about 15 minutes. Remove your vanilla bean.

3. In your stand mixer fitted with the whisk attachment or using a hand mixer, whip your cream to soft peaks. Add your yogurt and continue whipping on a medium-high until very thick. Should take about 1 minute. With your mixer running, slowly pour your cooled syrup down the side of your bowl. Whip for 2 minutes longer to incorporate plenty of air. The mousse will be fluffy, but will not hold a firm peak.

4. Divide among 4 dessert glasses or small bowls. Cover and chill until very cold. Approximately 2 to 4 hours.

5. In your small-sized saucepan, combine your balsamic vinegar, honey, and 1/4 teaspoon of pepper. Set over a medium heat. Bring to a boil, stirring for the first minute to dissolve your honey. Continue boiling, swirling your pan, until your syrup is reduced to 1 to 2 tablespoons. Should take approximately 3 to 4 minutes. It will be thick and sticky. Scrape over your berries, and stir gently to coat.

6. Divide your balsamic berries among your mousse glasses. Garnish each of your servings with a crumbled amaretti cookie.

7. Serve!

Taralli Baresi

Ingredients:

2 1/2 pounds of Flour

1-ounce of Fresh Yeast

1 cup of White Wine

1 cup of Olive Oil

1 cup of Water

1 tablespoon of Salt

Directions:

1. In your stand mixer bowl, combine all your liquids, yeast, and salt. Mix together well.

2. Add your flour and mix well until all your ingredients are well amalgamated.

3. Cut a chunk of dough about the size of a baseball and pass it through your pasta roller attachment of your stand mixer. Repeat the process 20 times for each piece to ensure that your dough is well mixed and all the air bubbles are removed.

4. Roll your dough into an 8-inch round shape that is about 1/2-inch thick.

5. Unite and press both ends to form a round taralli. Make all your taralli.

6. Take a few taralli at a time and boil them in your water. When you place your taralli in your boiling water they will sink to the bottom of your pan and may tend to stick to the bottom. With a wooden spoon, move them gently to remove them from the bottom. When they come up to the surface, remove them from the water and put them on your cloth to dry.

7. After you've boiled all your taralli, with a blade, make an incision all around the outer surface of each taralli 1/4-inch deep.

8. Place all your taralli on your baking sheet and bake them for approximately 7 minutes at 475 degrees. Lower your temperature to 400 degrees and continue baking them for an additional 20 minutes.

9. Halfway through your baking process, flip all your taralli so that they color evenly on both sides.

10. After you have baked all your taralli, put all your taralli in your baking pan and put them in your oven one more time for approximately 30 minutes at 180 degrees. This will ensure that all the moisture is removed from your taralli and will allow them to stay crispy.

11. Serve!

Kataifi (Serves 10)

Ingredients:

1/2 pound of Kataifi Phyllo

2 Eggs

2 pounds of Blanched & Chopped Almonds

1 teaspoon of Cinnamon

1 3/4 cups of Butter

4 tablespoons of Sugar

Syrup:

5 cups of Water

1 Lemon Rind

1 teaspoon of Lemon Juice

1 1/2 Kilogram of Sugar

Directions:

1. Preheat your oven to 350 degrees.

2. Put your almonds in your bowl with your sugar, cinnamon, and eggs.

3. Gently open your kataifi pastry with your fingers, lay it on a piece of wood or marble and put one tablespoonful of your almond mixture on one end, then roll your kataifi pastry into a cylinder.

3. Take care to fold your pastry a little tight at first so that your filling is securely enclosed.

4. Put it in your buttered baking dish.

5. Melt your butter and cover every piece of rolled kataifi with it.

6. Bake in your oven for approximately 30 minutes.

7. Meanwhile, prepare your syrup. Cook your sugar with the water and lemon rind for 5 to 10 minutes.

8. Add your lemon juice and leave to cook briefly until your syrup becomes thick.

9. After removing your kataifi from your oven and before it becomes cold, pour your syrup over it.

10. Cover your pastry with a clean towel and leave it to cool as it absorbs your syrup.

11. Serve!

Strained Yogurt

Ingredients:

1 quart of 2% Milk

1 pouch of Freeze Dried Yogurt Cultures

Large piece of Cheesecloth

Directions:

1. Heat your oven to 200 degrees for approximately 10 minutes; then turn it off.

2. Heat your milk over a medium heat on your stove top. Bring it to a boil and watch it closely as it begins to rise up in your pan.

3. Remove from your heat and pour into your ceramic bowl on your counter. Allow it to cool to approximately 110 degrees Fahrenheit or until you can insert your finger without getting burned.

4. Stir in your cultures and cover your bowl with plastic wrap.

5. Set your bowl in your warmed up oven for approximately 6 to 8 hours to allow your cultures to grow.

6. Remove your bowl from your oven and transfer it to your refrigerator for approximately 4 to 6 hours.

7. Pour your yogurt into your large-sized piece of cheesecloth and allow any excess liquid to drain into your sink. Twist the top of your cheesecloth closed and hang your pouch from the faucet to allow it to continue draining for approximately 10 minutes. The longer your yogurt drains, the thicker it will become.

8. Serve!

Baked Quince in Red Wine (Serves 10)

Ingredients:

5 Large Pommes De Cydon Quinces

1 1/2 cups of Red Wine

2 Cinnamon Sticks

1 1/2 cups of Sugar

Directions:

1. Peel your quinces, removing your seeds and cut them in half.

2. Preheat your oven to 350 degrees.

3. Place your quinces in your baking tin facing down.

4. Pour enough water to cover them.

5. Add your sugar, cinnamon sticks, and wine to your baking tin.

6. Bake your quince for approximately 35 to 40 minutes until soft.

7. Allow them to chill and keep them in their syrup.

8. Serve!

Peloponnesian Diples (Serves 40)

Ingredients:

3 Eggs

3 cups of All Purpose Flour

2 tablespoons of Sugar

1 teaspoon of Baking Powder

1 Small Cup of Raki

Chopped Walnuts

Cinnamon

Honey Syrup:

3 cups of Sugar

3 cups of Water

1 Kilogram of Thyme Honey

1 package of Vanilla

1 Small Glass of Rum

Directions:

1. In your bowl sift your flour with your baking powder. Make a puddle in the middle and place your eggs, raki, and sugar.

2. Knead well until your dough becomes smooth and suitable to open your phyllo. Leave your dough for about 30 minutes to rest.

3. Cut your dough into pieces and place them on a surface that has been sprinkled with some flour so that your phyllo won't stick.

4. Sprinkle some flour on top so that your phyllo won't stick to your rolling pin and then roll open your phyllo.

5. Once you've opened your phyllo, cut vertical and horizontal stripes to create a small rectangular shaped phyllo.

6. With your small brush remove any of the remaining flour on top of your phyllo.

7. Warm your oil in your skillet and fry them.

8. With your forks, fold them twice while frying, making sure they remain golden colored and don't burn.

9. Take them out of your skillet and place them on your baking sheet.

10. Once all your diples have been fried prepare your syrup.

11. In your pot, boil your honey along with your sugar and water for about 10 minutes. Towards the end add your rum and vanilla.

12. Remove the foamy part of your syrup and lower your temperature by half. Dip your diples in your syrup and leave for a few minutes.

13. Remove from the syrup and place them on your tray. Sprinkle with your cinnamon and chopped walnuts.

14. Serve!

Honey-Spice Walnut Tart (Serves 10)

Ingredients:

1 Large Egg

2 tablespoons of Granulated Sugar

4 tablespoons of Unsalted Butter

1/3 cup of Honey

1 1/2 teaspoons of Ground Cinnamon

1 cup of Roughly Chopped Walnuts

1 teaspoon of Ground Ginger

1 sheet of Frozen Puff Pastry (9 Ounces)

Salt

Directions:

1. Heat your oven to 400 degrees. In your food processor, blend your butter, honey, cinnamon, salt, sugar, and ginger until smooth. Add your egg and process until well blended. Add your nuts all at once and process only until blended. The nuts should be chopped, but not so fine that your mixture becomes a smooth paste.

2. Cut your pastry sheet in half to make 2 strips about 9x4-inches. Roll one strip to 15x6-inches. Prick the entire surface of your strip with the tines of your fork. Slide your sheet onto a parchment-lined baking sheet. Spread the center of your strip with half of your nut mixture, to within 1/2-inch of the long edges and all the way to the edge on the short ends. Fold the bare long edges 1/2-inch over your nut mixture and press firmly to stick. With the blunt edge of your table knife, make indentations into the long edges about 1/2-inch apart to crimp the border a bit. Repeat with your second pastry strip and the rest of your nut mixture.

3. Bake in your heated oven until your filling looks slightly dry on top and your pastry is a deep golden brown on the edges and underneath. Should take approximately 19 to 21 minutes. Slide your tarts onto a rack to cool. Cut into four or five strips each and serve slightly warm.

4. Serve!

Sangria Granita (Serves)

Ingredients:

3/4 cup of Wine

1/4 cup of Fresh Orange Juice

1/4 cup + 2 tablespoons of Granulated Sugar

2 tablespoons of Fresh Lemon Juice

Directions:

1. Combine your red wine, 1/2 cup water, and sugar in your medium-sized saucepan. Bring to a boil over a medium heat. Boil for approximately 1 minute. Remove your pan from the heat and stir in your orange and lemon juice. Allow it to cool.

2. Pour your wine mixture into a 9-inch-square shallow baking pan. This pan size works best because it provides a large surface area, a key point in speeding up the freezing process. To further hasten freezing, use a metal pan.

3. Put your pan in your freezer and stir every 30 minutes. Be sure to scrape the ice crystals off the sides and into the middle of your pan until the mixture is too frozen to stir. Should take about 3 hours, depending on the individual recipe and on how cold your freezer is. Use your large dinner fork to stir and scrape. The tines are ideal for breaking up ice crystals.

4. Cover your pan with plastic and freeze overnight. When ready to serve your granita, place your fork at the top of your dish and pull it toward you in rows, moving from left to right and rotating the pan as well. Scrape up your shaved ice and fill your chilled glasses or bowls.

5. Serve!

Conclusion

Thanks for reading my book. I hope this Mediterranean diet recipe guide has provided you with enough options to get you going. Don't put off getting started. The sooner you begin this diet the sooner you'll start to notice an improvement in your overall health and well-being. It's never too early to begin caring about your body and the health of your heart. While you won't see results overnight, they will come eventually.

There's no shortage of meals you can enjoy on a Mediterranean diet. I've tried to include a good variety of wonderful dishes so you can see if this diet is right for you.

Made in the USA
Middletown, DE
13 January 2018